⊙ April 15th 9:30

⊙ April 15th   11:59 →
                 7:46 am

Gate #2
Seat 23 A/B   out
Seat 25 A/B   in

Customer Focused Quality

FOR _____

CALLER _____

OF _____

PHONE ( ) _____ EXT. _____

☐ RETURNED YOUR CALL

☐ PLEASE CALL   HIM   HER

☐ WILL CALL AGAIN

MESSAGE _____

_____

_____

_____

_____

_____

Receiving

Keeping   Understanding

Helping

a.m. p.m.		
TIME	DATE	INITIALS

QUALITY IN ALL THAT WE DO

G111-12

Mini Las Vegas

the
Pocket-Sized Unofficial Guide® to Las Vegas

1st Edition

Also available from IDG Books Worldwide, Inc.:

Beyond Disney: The Unofficial Guide to Universal, Sea World, and the Best of Central Florida, by Bob Sehlinger and Amber Morris

Inside Disney: The Incredible Story of Walt Disney World and the Man Behind the Mouse, by Eve Zibart

Mini-Mickey: The Pocket-Sized Unofficial Guide to Walt Disney World, by Bob Sehlinger

The Unofficial Guide to Bed & Breakfasts in New England, by Lea Lane

The Unofficial Guide to Bed & Breakfasts in the Northwest, by Sally O'Neal Coates

The Unofficial Guide to Branson, Missouri, by Bob Sehlinger and Eve Zibart

The Unofficial Guide to California with Kids, by Colleen Dunn Bates and Susan LaTempa

The Unofficial Guide to Chicago, by Joe Surkiewicz and Bob Sehlinger

The Unofficial Guide to Cruises, by Kay Showker with Bob Sehlinger

The Unofficial Guide to Disneyland, by Bob Sehlinger

The Unofficial Guide to Florida with Kids, by Pam Brandon

The Unofficial Guide to the Great Smoky and Blue Ridge Region, by Bob Sehlinger and Joe Surkiewicz

The Unofficial Guide to Las Vegas, by Bob Sehlinger

The Unofficial Guide to London, by Lesley Logan

The Unofficial Guide to Miami and the Keys, by Bob Sehlinger and Joe Surkiewicz

The Unofficial Guide to New Orleans, by Bob Sehlinger and Eve Zibart

The Unofficial Guide to New York City, by Eve Zibart and Bob Sehlinger with Jim Leff

The Unofficial Guide to Paris, by David Applefield

The Unofficial Guide to San Francisco, by Joe Surkiewicz and Bob Sehlinger with Richard Sterling

The Unofficial Guide to Skiing in the West, by Lito Tejada-Flores, Peter Shelton, Seth Masia, Ed Chauner, and Bob Sehlinger

The Unofficial Guide to Walt Disney World, by Bob Sehlinger

The Unofficial Guide to Walt Disney World for Grown-Ups, by Eve Zibart

The Unofficial Guide to Walt Disney World with Kids, by Bob Sehlinger

The Unofficial Guide to Washington, D.C., by Bob Sehlinger and Joe Surkiewicz with Eve Zibart

Mini Las Vegas

the Pocket-Sized Unofficial Guide® to Las Vegas

1st Edition

Bob Sehlinger

IDG BOOKS
WORLDWIDE

An International Data Group Company
Foster City, CA • Chicago, IL • Indianapolis, IN
New York, NY • Southlake, TX

Every effort has been made to ensure the accuracy of information throughout this book. Bear in mind, however, that prices, schedules, etc., are constantly changing. Readers should always verify information before making final plans.

IDG Books Worldwide, Inc.
An International Data Group Company
919 E. Hillsdale Blvd.
Suite 400
Foster City, CA 94404

Produced by Menasha Ridge Press

MACMILLAN is a registered trademark of Macmillan, Inc., a wholly owned subsidiary of IDG Books Worldwide, Inc. *UNOFFICIAL GUIDE* is a registered trademark of Macmillan, Inc., a wholly owned subsidiary of IDG Books Worldwide, Inc.

ISBN 0-02-863266-4
ISSN 1522-3353

Manufactured in the United States of America
10 9 8 7 6 5 4 3 2 1
First edition

Contents

List of Illustrations vii
Acknowledgments viii

Introduction

On a Plane to Las Vegas 1
About This Guide 3
How Information Is Organized: By Subject and
    by Geographic Zones 5
Las Vegas: An Overview 12
Arriving and Getting Oriented 15
Las Vegas as a Family Destination 21

I Lodging and Casinos

Where to Stay: Basic Choices 23
Getting Around: Location and Convenience 27
What's in an Address? 31
Room Reservations: Getting a Good Room, Getting a Good
    Deal 36
For Business Travelers 42
Comfort Zones: Matching Guests with Hotels 45
Hotels with Casinos 45
Suite Hotels 66
Suite Hotels without Casinos 66
Las Vegas Motels 67
Hotel-Casinos and Motels: Rated and Ranked 67
Leisure, Recreation, and Services Rating of Hotel-Casinos
    73
Putting the Ratings Together 78

2 Entertainment and Nightlife

Las Vegas Shows and Entertainment   81

Selecting a Show   88

The Best Shows in Town: Celebrity Headliners   89

Production Shows   93

Comedy Clubs   114

Las Vegas Nightlife   117

Las Vegas below the Belt   123

3 Gambling

The Way It Is   126

4 Shopping and Seeing the Sights

Shopping in Las Vegas   144

Seeing the Sights   146

Other Area Attractions   153

5 Dining and Restaurants

Dining in Las Vegas   155

The Restaurants   163

Index   210

Reader Survey   216

List of Illustrations

Regional Map of Nevada and the Intermountain West 2
Las Vegas Touring Zones 6
Zone 1 The Strip 7
Zone 2 Downtown 8
Zone 3 Southwest Las Vegas 9
Zone 4 North Las Vegas 10
Zone 5 Southeast Las Vegas and the Boulder Highway 11
Las Vegas Weather and Dress Chart 14
Clark County, Nevada & Surrounding Area 16
Hotels on or near the Strip 24
Downtown Las Vegas 26
Las Vegas Strip Walking Map 30
Hotel Clusters along the Strip 33
Strip Hotel Sneak Routes 35

Acknowledgments

The people of Las Vegas love their city and spare no effort to assist a writer trying to dig beneath the facade of flashing neon. It is important to them to communicate that Las Vegas is a city with depth, diversity, and substance. "Don't just write about our casinos," they demand, "take the time to get to know us."

We made every effort to do just that, enabled each step of the way by some of the most sincere and energetic folks a writer could hope to encounter. Myram Borders of the Las Vegas News Bureau provided us access to anyone we wanted to see, from casino general managers to vice cops. Cam Usher of the Las Vegas Convention and Visitors Authority also spared no effort in offering assistance and contacts. Thanks to Nevada expert Deke Castleman for his contributions to our entertainment, nightlife, buffet, and hotel coverage.

Restaurant critic Muriel Stevens ate her way through dozens of new restaurants but drew the line when it came to buffet duty. Jim McDonald of the Las Vegas Police Department shared his experiences and offered valuable suggestions for staying out of trouble. Jack Sheehan evaluated Las Vegas golf courses, and forest ranger Debbie Savage assisted us in developing material on wilderness recreation.

Purple Hearts to our field research team, who chowed down on every buffet and $2 steak in town, checked in and out of countless hotels, visited tourist attractions, and stood for hours in show lines:

Mike Jones	K'-Lynne Cotton	Nicole Jones	Marty Newey
Julie Newey	Holly Cross	Shirley Gutke	Dan Cotton
Joan Burns	Lee Wiseman	Molly Burns	Leslie Cummins
Grace Walton	Sean Ross		

Much gratitude to Holly Cross, Molly Harrison, Chris Crochetière, Barbara Williams, Julie Allred, Brian Taylor, and Ann Cassar, the pros who somehow turned all this effort into a book.

Introduction

On a Plane to Las Vegas

I never wanted to go to Las Vegas. I'm not much of a gambler, and I always thought of Las Vegas as dedicated to separating folks from their money. But I'm involved with industries that hold conventions and trade shows there. For years I was able to persuade others to go in my place. Eventually, I found myself aboard a jet bound for Las Vegas.

Passengers around me were in two camps. Some thought themselves on a flight to nirvana. They roamed the aisles clapping one another on the back in excitement. Other passengers wore sour expressions. They lamented their trip to such a place.

And me? To my surprise, I had a great time without gambling, and I've been back many times without a bad experience. People are friendly, food is good, hotels are a bargain, it's easy to get around, and there's plenty to do at any hour.

I've discovered that nongamblers know little about Las Vegas. Many, plus people only marginally interested in gambling, see scant value beyond the gambling. But sun worshipers find fine food and resorts, golf, sightseeing, shopping, and theater. Nature lovers savor nearby areas. And all of it is at probably the lowest prices anywhere. Gambling is just the tip of the iceberg.

This guide is for those who want to go to Las Vegas and for those who *have* to go to Las Vegas. If you are a recreational gambler and/or enthusiastic vacationer, we'll help you pour champagne over the iceberg. We'll show you ways to have more fun, make the most of your time, and spend less. If you're a skeptic, an unwilling companion of gamblers, a business traveler, or just someone wishing they were someplace else, we'll help you discover the

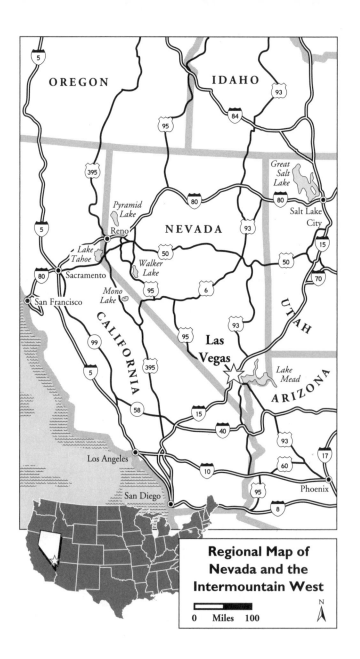

Regional Map of Nevada and the Intermountain West

0   Miles   100

N

hidden nine-tenths of Las Vegas. We'll demonstrate that you can have the time of your life in this friendly city and never bet that first nickel.

About This Guide

How Come "Unofficial"?

Most "official" guides to Las Vegas tout the well-known sights, promote local casinos, restaurants, and hotels indiscriminately, and leave out a lot of good stuff. This guide is different.

Instead of pandering to the tourism industry, we'll tell you if a well-known restaurant's food is mediocre. We'll complain loudly about overpriced hotel rooms that aren't convenient to the places you want to be, and we'll guide you away from crowds and congestion.

Our evaluators toured the casinos and popular attractions, reviewed the shows, ate in the restaurants, judged hotels, and visited nightclubs. If a restaurant's food is bad or a show isn't worth the admission, we can say so—and, in the process, make your visit more fun, efficient, and economical.

Creating a Guidebook

We got into the guidebook business because we were unhappy with the way travel guides make the reader work for usable information.

Most guidebooks are compilations of lists presented in list form or prose. Because lists offer insufficient detail, such guides provide little more than departure points for readers' further quests.

Many guides are readable and well researched but difficult to use. To select a hotel, for example, a reader must study several pages of descriptions before narrowing their choices. If recommendations are made, they lack depth and conviction. These guides compound problems by failing to boil down travelers' choices.

How Unofficial Guides Are Different

Readers want the author's opinion and quick answers. This dictates that authors should be explicit, prescriptive, and direct. The *Unofficial Guides* try to do that. They spell out alternatives and recommend specific action, as well as simplifying complicated destinations and attractions and helping the traveler control unfamiliar environments. The objective of an *Unofficial Guide* is not to have the most information or all of the information, but to have the most accessible, useful, and unbiased information.

Unofficial Guide authors and researchers are completely independent from the attractions, restaurants, and hotels we describe. *The Unofficial Guide to Las Vegas* is designed for individuals and families traveling for fun, as well as for business travelers and convention-goers, especially those visiting Las Vegas for the first time. The guide is directed at value-conscious, consumer-oriented adults.

How This Guide Was Researched and Written

Much has been written about Las Vegas, but very little has been evaluative. Some guides regurgitate the hotels' and casinos' promotional material. In this work, we took nothing for granted. Each casino, hotel, restaurant, show, and attraction was visited at different times throughout the year by trained observers. They conducted detailed evaluations and rated each property and entertainment according to formal, pretested criteria. Tourists were interviewed to determine what visitors of all ages enjoyed most *and least.*

Observers used detailed checklists to analyze casinos, attractions, hotel rooms, buffets, and restaurants. Finally, ratings and observations were integrated with tourists' reactions and opinions for a comprehensive quality profile of each feature and service.

Letters, Comments, and Questions from Readers

We welcome questions and comments from *Unofficial Guides* readers. Their remarks frequently are incorporated in revised editions of the *Unofficial Guide*. The author's address:

Bob Sehlinger
The Unofficial Guide to Las Vegas
P.O. Box 43673
Birmingham, AL 35243
Please put your address on both your letter and envelope—the

two sometimes become separated. And remember: Our work takes us out of the office for long periods. Our response may be delayed.

Reader Survey

At the back of this guide is a questionnaire on your Las Vegas visit. Clip the completed questionnaire and mail it to the author.

HOW INFORMATION IS ORGANIZED: BY SUBJECT AND BY GEOGRAPHIC ZONES

To provide fast access to information about the *best* of Las Vegas, we've organized material in several formats.

Hotels Because most visitors stay in one hotel for the duration of their trip, our coverage of hotels is summarized in charts, maps, ratings, and rankings that allow you to quickly focus your decision-making. We concentrate on specifics that differentiate hotels: location, size, room quality, services, amenities, and cost.

Restaurants We profile the best restaurants.

Entertainment and Nightlife Visitors frequently try several shows or nightspots. Because these are usually selected after arrival, we offer detailed descriptions. All continuous stage shows and celebrity showrooms are reviewed. The best nightspots and lounges are profiled (pages 117–23).

Geographic Zones To help you locate restaurants, shows, nightspots, and attractions convenient to your hotel, we divide the city into geographic zones:

- Zone 1 The Las Vegas Strip and Environs
- Zone 2 Downtown Las Vegas
- Zone 3 Southwest Las Vegas
- Zone 4 North Las Vegas
- Zone 5 Southeast Las Vegas and the Boulder Highway

All profiles of hotels, restaurants, and nightspots include zone numbers. If, for example, you're staying at the Golden Nugget and want an Italian restaurant within walking distance, scan the restaurant profiles for restaurants in Zone 2 (downtown) for the best choices.

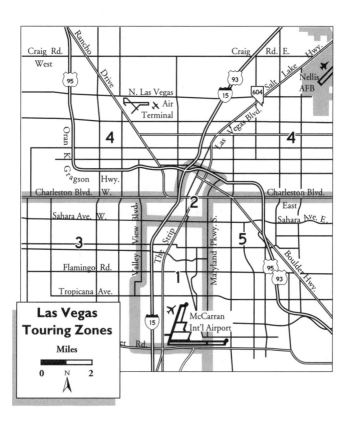

Craig Rd.
West

Craig Rd. E.

Rancho Drive

95

93

15

604

Salt Lake Hwy.

Nellis
AFB

N. Las Vegas
Air
Terminal

Las Vegas Blvd.

Oran K. Gragson Hwy.

4

4

Charleston Blvd. W.

Charleston Blvd.

Sahara Ave. W.

East
Sahara Ave. E.

Valley View Blvd.

The Strip

Maryland Pkwy. S.

3

5

2

Flamingo Rd.

95

Boulder Hwy.

1

93

Tropicana Ave.

Las Vegas
Touring Zones

Miles

0   N   2

McCarran
Int'l Airport

15

Rd.

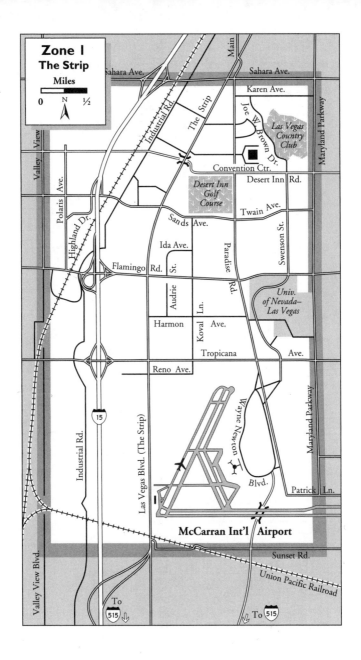

Zone I
The Strip

Miles

0   N   ½

Sahara Ave.

Sahara Ave.

Karen Ave.

The Strip

Joe W. Brown Dr.

Las Vegas Country Club

Maryland Parkway

Valley View

Industrial Rd.

Convention Ctr.

Desert Inn Rd.

Desert Inn Golf Course

Polaris Ave.

Highland Dr.

Sands Ave.

Twain Ave.

Swenson St.

Ida Ave.

Paradise Rd.

Flamingo Rd.

St.

Audrie Ln.

Univ. of Nevada–Las Vegas

Harmon

Koval Ave.

Tropicana   Ave.

Reno Ave.

Maryland Parkway

15

Industrial Rd.

Las Vegas Blvd. (The Strip)

Wayne Newton Blvd.

Patrick Ln.

I

McCarran Int'l Airport

Valley View Blvd.

Sunset Rd.

Union Pacific Railroad

To 515

To 515

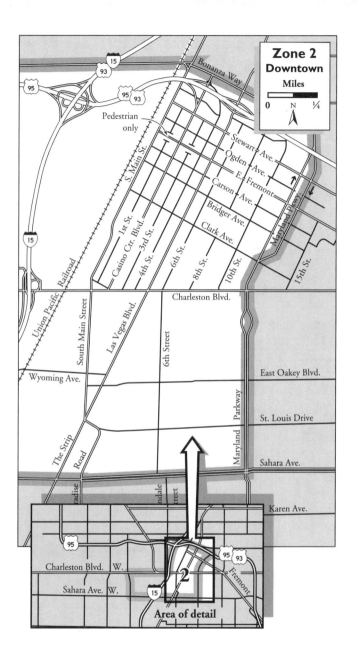

Zone 2
Downtown

Miles

0   N   ¼

Bonanza Way

Pedestrian only

Stewart Ave.
Ogden Ave.
E. Fremont
Carson Ave.
Bridger Ave.
Clark Ave.

S. Main St.
1st St.
Casino Ctr. Blvd.
3rd St.
4th St.
6th St.
8th St.
10th St.
15th St.

Maryland Pkwy.

Union Pacific Railroad

Charleston Blvd.

South Main Street

Las Vegas Blvd.

6th Street

Wyoming Ave.

East Oakey Blvd.

St. Louis Drive

Maryland Parkway

Sahara Ave.

The Strip

Paradise Road

...ndale Street

Karen Ave.

Charleston Blvd. W.

Sahara Ave. W.

Fremont

2

Area of detail

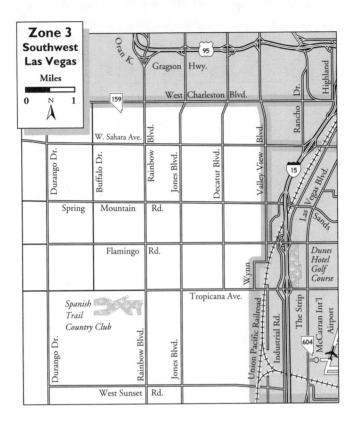

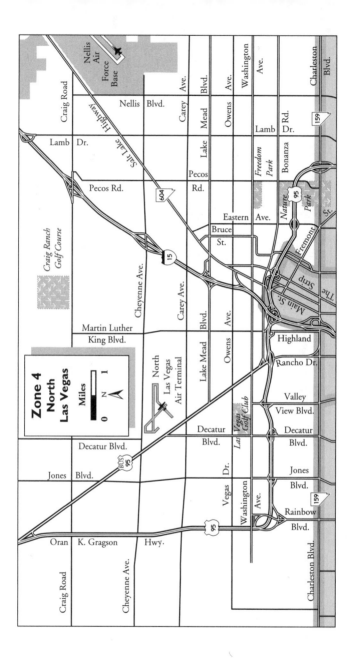

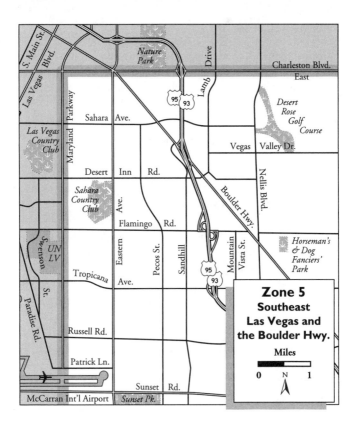

S. Main St.

Las Vegas Blvd.

Nature Park

Drive

Charleston Blvd.

East

Maryland Parkway

Sahara Ave.

95 93

Lamb

Desert Rose Golf Course

Las Vegas Country Club

Vegas Valley Dr.

Desert Inn Rd.

Sahara Country Club

Nellis Blvd.

Ave.

Boulder Hwy.

Flamingo Rd.

S. Swenson St.

UN LV

Eastern

Pecos St.

Sandhill

Mountain Vista St.

Horseman's & Dog Fanciers' Park

Paradise Rd.

Tropicana Ave.

95
93

Zone 5
Southeast
Las Vegas and
the Boulder Hwy.

Russell Rd.

Miles

Patrick Ln.

0   N   1

McCarran Int'l Airport

Sunset Rd.

Sunset Pk.

11

Comfort Zones   Every Las Vegas hotel-casino has its own personality and clientele. To help you find the hotel-casino where you will feel most at home, we describe the patron of each. Descriptions begin on page 45.

Las Vegas: An Overview

GATHERING INFORMATION

Las Vegas has the best selection of free visitor guides of any American tourist destination we know. Available at the front desk or concierge table at almost every hotel, the guides provide useful information on gaming, gambling lessons, shows, lounge entertainment, sports, buffets, meal deals, tours, sightseeing, transportation, shopping, and special events. Most contain coupons for discounts on dining, shows, attractions, and tours.

Today in Las Vegas is the most comprehensive of these guides. *Tourguide Magazine of Las Vegas* is also very comprehensive. In *Today*, restaurants are listed by type (buffets, brunches, steak, Italian), while restaurants in *Tourguide* are listed alphabetically by host casino. Because both formats are handy, we recommend picking up a copy of each magazine.

Both are published weekly and are free. For a copy before you arrive, contact:

Today in Las Vegas
Lycoria Publishing Company
3626 Pecos McCleod Drive, Suite 14
Las Vegas, NV 89121
(702) 385-2737

Tourguide Magazine of Las Vegas
4440 S. Arville St., Suite 12
Las Vegas, NV 89103
(702) 221-5000

Other weeklies are *Showbiz Magazine,* published by the *Las Vegas Sun* newspaper, and *What's On in Las Vegas.* Both also include weekly television listings. *Showbiz* and *What's On* are generally in hotel guest rooms.

The monthly *Las Vegas Advisor* newsletter contains some of the most useful consumer information available on gaming, dining, and entertainment, as well as details of deals on rooms, drinks, shows, and meals. With no advertising or promotional content, the newsletter offers objective, no-nonsense advice. Subscriptions are $50 a year. Single copies are $5 at the Gambler's Book Club store at 630 S. 11th St., (702) 382-7555. For additional information, write:

Las Vegas Advisor
Huntington Press
3687 S. Procyon Ave., Suite A
Las Vegas, NV 89103
(702) 252-0655
(800) 244-2224

Las Vegas and the Internet

Here are the best Las Vegas sites on the World Wide Web (use directories to surf individual sites):

The (almost) Ultimate Guide to Las Vegas Internet Addresses is at www.infi.net/vegas.

The official Web site of the Las Vegas Convention and Visitors Authority is www.lasvegas.24hours.com.

For the largest selection of casinos, go to intermind.net, then hit Hotels & Casinos.

Other Las Vegas On-Ramps include:

www.vegas.com
www.earthlink.net
www.pcap.com.

WHEN TO GO TO LAS VEGAS

The best time to go to Las Vegas is spring or fall, when the weather is pleasant. If you plan to be indoors, it doesn't matter when you go. Spring and fall are the most popular, but the best deals are in December (after the National Finals Rodeo in early December and excluding the week between Christmas and New Year's), January, and during summer, particularly July and August.

Weather in December, January, and February can vary incredibly, but chances are better than even that temperatures will be moderate and the sun will shine. Winter provides an unbeatable combination of good value and choice of activities. From mid-May through mid-September, the heat is blistering.

LAS VEGAS WEATHER AND DRESS CHART				
Month	**Average a.m. Temp.**	**Average p.m. Temp.**	**Pools O=Open**	**Recommended Attire**
January	57	32		Coats and jackets are a must.
February	50	37		Dress warmly: jackets and sweaters.
March	69	42	/O	Sweaters for days, but a jacket at night.
April	78	50	O	Still cool at night—bring a jacket.
May	88	50	O	Sweater for evening, but days are warm.
June	99	68	O	Days hot and evenings are moderate.
July	105	75	O	Bathing suits.
August	102	73	O	Dress for the heat—spend time at a pool!
September	95	65	O	Days warm, sweater for evening.
October	81	53	O/	Bring a jacket or sweater for p.m.
November	67	40		Sweaters and jackets, coats for night.
December	58	34		Coats and jackets a must: dress warmly!

Avoiding Crowds

Weekends generally are busy; weekdays, slower. Exceptions are holiday periods and when large conventions or special events are being held. (Two or three concurrent medium-sized conventions can impact Las Vegas as much as one citywide event.) Most hotels' rates are lower on weekdays. For a stress-free arrival at the airport; good availability of rental cars; and quick hotel check-in, arrive Monday afternoon through Thursday morning (Tuesday and Wednesday are best).

Las Vegas hosts huge conventions and special events (rodeos, prizefights) that tie up hotels, restaurants, transportation, showrooms, and traffic for a week at a time. For a complete convention calendar, call the Las Vegas Convention and Visitors Authority at (702) 892-0711.

Arriving and Getting Oriented

If you drive, you will cross the desert to reach Las Vegas. Make sure your car is in good shape, and carry a couple of gallons of water for emergencies. Monitor fuel and temperature gauges.

Virtually all commercial air traffic uses McCarran International Airport, a well-designed facility with clear signs. You will have no problem navigating, but the walk to baggage claim can be long. Baggage handling is slow. While your checked luggage is en route, complete paperwork at nearby car rental counters. Have your baggage claim check handy; you'll have to show it.

Not renting a car? No problem. Shuttles to hotels start at $3.75 one way and $8 round trip. Sedans and "stretch" limousines cost about $25 to $33 one way. Cabs are also available; the fare to Strip locations is about $9 to $18 one way, plus tip. A cab to downtown is about $16 to $23 one way. Limo service counters are just outside baggage claim; cabs are at the curb.

If you rent a car, catch your rental company's courtesy vehicle at the middle curb of the authorized vehicle lanes (ground level between the baggage claim building and the terminal).

If someone is picking you up, proceed on ground level to the opposite side of the baggage claim building (away from the main terminal) to the baggage claim/arrivals curb. If the person picking you up wants to park, meet on the ground level of the baggage claim building near the car rental counters where the escalators descend from the main terminal.

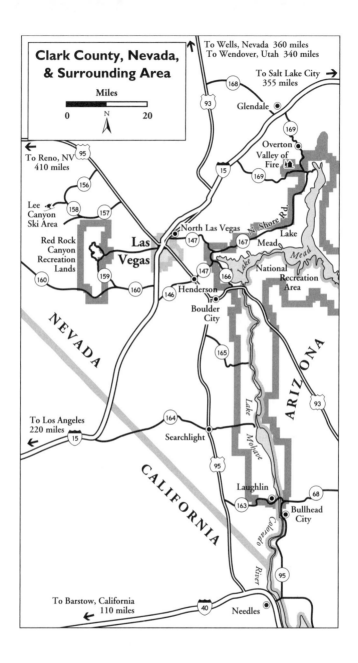

Clark County, Nevada,
& Surrounding Area

Miles

0   N   20

To Wells, Nevada 360 miles
To Wendover, Utah 340 miles

To Salt Lake City →
355 miles

168

93

Glendale ◉

169

Overton ●
Valley of
Fire ⛺

← To Reno, NV
410 miles

95

15

169

156

158   157

Lee
Canyon
Ski Area

North Las Vegas ●

147

N. Shore Rd.

Lake
Mead

Las
Vegas

167

Red Rock
Canyon
Recreation
Lands

159

147

166

Lake

Mead

National
Recreation
Area

160

160

146

Henderson ●

Boulder
City ●

NEVADA

165

ARIZONA

To Los Angeles
220 miles

15

164

Searchlight ●

95

Lake Mohave

93

CALIFORNIA

Laughlin ●

163

68

Bullhead
City ●

Colorado

95

To Barstow, California
110 miles
←

40

Needles ●

River

By car, leave the airport via Swenson Street, which runs north-south roughly paralleling the Strip, or take the spur of Interstate 515, which connects with I-15. We recommend I-515 if you're headed downtown or to hotels west of the Strip. Swenson Street is better if you're going to the Las Vegas Convention Center, UNLV, or hotels on or east of the Strip.

Convenience Chart   We've included a chart of estimated times by foot and cab from 50 major hotels to popular destinations plus tips for avoiding traffic between the Strip and downtown.

Rental Cars   All national car rental companies and a few local firms serve the city. Agencies with counters at McCarran process customers faster than do off-airport sites, which also require a commute to their location. (Courtesy vehicles pick up at the center curb outside baggage claim.) The county charges 8% of your rental fee if you use an off-airport agency. With 7% sales tax, 6% state surcharge, and 8% airport fee, rental car taxes can add 21% to your bill.

Prices fluctuate; have your travel agent check rates at all rental agencies for the dates of your visit. On many weekends or when a citywide convention is in town, rental cars may be unavailable unless you reserved in advance. When business is slow, rentals may go for as little as $22 a day. In slow seasons, reserve ahead but check each company on arrival. You may find a better deal.

Rental Car Agencies	
At the Terminal	**Off-Airport**
Ace	Alamo
Airpot Car Rental	Enterprise
All State	Ladki International
Avis	Practical
Budget	Resort
Dollar	Thrifty
Hertz	US RentCar
National	
Savmor	

When you or your travel agent reserve a rental car, ask for the smallest and least expensive (you may be upgraded without charge on arrival). Or, agencies frequently offer on-site upgrades that beat any advance deals. Always compare daily and weekly rates.

If you decline insurance coverage on the rental car, be clear what protection your credit card provides and how your regular auto insurance covers you. In most cases, credit card coverage reimburses you only the deductible on your regular policy. If you decline coverage, inspect the vehicle very carefully for any damage (even a windshield nick) and have the agent record any blemish. Among credit cards, Diner's Club offers the best supplemental coverage.

Some agencies require that you drive only in Nevada. If you visit Hoover Dam or the Grand Canyon, you will cross into Arizona. Also, your agency may charge for additional drivers.

Return the car with a full gas tank. Some companies charge $3 or more per gallon for gas. The price for a fill-up on return will be on your rental contract.

Public Transportation   Las Vegas's Citizen's Area Transit (CAT) provides reliable bus service at reasonable rates. One-way fares along the Strip are $1.50. Children ages five and younger ride free. Exact fare is required. Transfers are free but must be used within one hour of issue. Handicapped persons requiring door-to-door service should call ahead for reservations. For more details, call (702) 228-7433.

The privately owned Las Vegas Strip Trolley Company provides transportation on the Strip and between the Strip and downtown. Its buses mimic San Francisco cable cars, and the fare is less than on CAT buses. Children ages four and younger ride free. Call (702) 382-1404 for information.

Las Vegas Customs and Protocol

The only rules for being accepted in Las Vegas are these: Have a shirt on your back, shoes on your feet, clothing below the waist, and money in your pocket (the minimum is fare back to wherever you came from).

After that, there are three areas where the uninitiated feel insecure:

Gambling   Despite appearances, gambling is very informal. It's smart to avoid a game you don't know how to play, but uncertainty over the protocol shouldn't stop you. What little protocol exists (including holding your cards above the table and keeping your hands away from your bet once play has begun) has evolved to protect the house and honest players from cheats. Dealers (those who conduct table games) aren't ordered to be unfriendly or silent. Before you sit down, find a game that interests you and observe that the dealer is personable and polite. Never play where the staff is surly; life's too short.

Eating in Gourmet Restaurants   Don't be intimidated. These are mostly meat and potatoes places with fancy names. Men will feel more comfortable in sport coats; ties are optional. Women wear everything from slacks to evening attire. When you sit down, a platoon of waiters will attend you. Let the waiter put your napkin in your lap. Then, the senior waiter speaks. Afterward, you may order cocktails, consider the menu, sip your water, or converse. Women in a mixed party will receive a menu without prices. In an all-woman party, a menu with prices will be given to the woman who looks oldest.

There will be enough utensils on the table to perform surgery. Use a different one for each dish, and let the waiter take it at the end of the course. Small yellow sculptures are probably butter.

Tipping   Las Vegas has no scarcity of people to tip. Remember that a tip isn't automatic—it rewards good service. Here are traditional amounts:

Porters and Redcaps   A dollar a bag.

Cab Drivers   Give weight to service and courtesy. If the fare is less than $8, give the cabbie the change and $1. For example, on a $4.50 fare, give him the 50 cents change plus a buck. If the fare is more than $8, give him the change and $2. On trips of only

---

Sound Like an Old-Timer

Never refer to Las Vegas as "Vegas."

a block or two, the fare will be small, but your tip should be large ($3–5) to compensate the cabbie for his wait in line and missing a better-paying fare. Tip an extra dollar if the cabbie handles a lot of luggage.

Valet Parking   Two dollars is correct if the valet is courteous and demonstrates hustle. A dollar will do if the service is just OK. Pay only when you retrieve your car. Attendants pool their tips, so both individuals who assist you (coming and going) will be taken care of.

Bellhops   If a bellman greets you at your car with a rolling cart and handles all of your bags, $5 is about right. The more luggage you carry yourself, the less you should tip.

Waiters   Whether in a coffee shop or gourmet room, or ordering from room service, the standard gratuity for acceptable service is 15% of the tab, before sales tax. At a buffet, leave $1–2 for the person who brings your drinks.

Cocktail Waiters/Bartenders   Tip by the round. For two people, $1 a round; for more than two people, $2 a round. For a large group, use your judgment: Is everyone drinking beer, or is the order long and complicated? In casinos where drinks are free, tip the server $1 per round or every couple of rounds.

Dealers and Slot Attendants   If you're winning, tip the dealer or place a small bet for him. How much depends on your winnings and level of play. With slot attendants, tip when they perform a service (like turning you on to a loose machine), or when you hit a jackpot. It isn't customary to tip change makers or cashiers.

Keno Runners   Tip if you have a winner or if the runner is fast and efficient. How much depends on your winnings and level of play.

Showroom Maître d's, Captains, and Servers   If you're planning to see a show, read our suggestions for tipping in the chapter on entertainment.

Hotel Maids   On check-out, leave $1–2 for each day you stayed, providing the service was good.

DOES ANYONE KNOW WHAT'S GOING ON AT HOME? (DOES ANYONE REALLY CARE?)

Las Vegas International News Stand at 3900 Paradise Road stocks Sunday papers from most major cities. To learn if yours is among them, call (702) 796-9901.

Las Vegas as a Family Destination

Occasionally the publisher sends me touring to promote the *Unofficial Guide* on radio and television, and every year I am asked: Is Las Vegas a good place for a family vacation?

Objectively, Las Vegas is a great place for a family vacation. Food and lodging are a bargain, and there are many things the family can enjoy together. If you take your children to Las Vegas *and forget gambling,* Las Vegas compares favorably with every U.S. family tourist destination. The rub is that gambling is hard to ignore. (Remember: Persons younger than 21 aren't allowed to gamble or to hang around while *you* gamble.)

Marketing gurus have tried to recast the city as a family destination. The strategy attracts a few parents already drawn to gambling but previously unwilling to spend a family vacation in Las Vegas. But it takes a lot more than hype to convince most parents the city is suitable for a family vacation.

For years, Las Vegas has been touted as a place to *get away* from the kids. For family tourism to succeed, that characterization has to be changed or minimized. Next, gambling must be relegated to secondary importance. Las Vegas can't be a bona fide family destination until something supersedes gambling as the main draw. Not very likely. The MGM Grand Adventures Theme Park and Adventuredome at Circus Circus represent a start, but they're only a start.

To legitimately appeal to families, the city must consider the real needs of children and parents. Instead of banishing children to midway and electronic games arcades, hotels need to offer substantive, educational, supervised programs or "camps" for children. The Station casinos are breaking ground in this area. Equally important, Las Vegas must sell itself in new geographic areas. Southern California is Las Vegas's most lucrative market, but it's not reasonable to expect families with Disneyland, Sea World, and Universal Studios to go to Las Vegas for a theme park.

Tours and Excursions

Bus sightseeing tours offer two things: transportation and drivers who know where they're going. If you have a car and can read a map, save money and hassle by going on your own.

Special Events

There is almost always something fun going on besides gambling: minor league baseball, rodeos, concerts, UNLV basketball and football, and, of course, movies. Buy a local newspaper and check the listings.

Part One

Lodging and Casinos

Where to Stay: Basic Choices

THE LAS VEGAS STRIP AND DOWNTOWN

From a visitor's perspective, Las Vegas is a small town and fairly easy to navigate. Most major hotels and casinos are in two areas: downtown and on Las Vegas Boulevard, known as the Strip.

Downtown hotels and casinos are generally older and smaller than those on the Strip, but there are large and elegant hotels downtown. What differentiates downtown is the incredible concentration of casinos and hotels in a relatively small area. Along four blocks of Fremont Street, downtown's main thoroughfare, the casinos present a dazzling galaxy of neon and twinkling lights known as Glitter Gulch. Several dozen casinos are sandwiched into an area barely larger than the parking lot at a good-sized shopping mall.

Downtown has the atmosphere of New Orleans's Bourbon Street: alluring, exotic, wicked, sultry, foreign, and, above all, diverse. It's where cowboy, businessperson, showgirl, and retiree mix easily. And like Bourbon Street, it's accessible on foot.

If downtown is the French Quarter, then the Strip is Plantation Row. At its heart, huge hotel-casinos sprawl like estates along four miles of Las Vegas Boulevard South. Each hotel is a vacation destination unto itself, with casino, hotel, restaurants, pools, spas, landscaped grounds, and even golf courses.

Considered part of the Strip is the Paradise Road area east and parallel to the Strip where the Las Vegas Convention Center and several hotels are located. Also included are hotels and casinos on

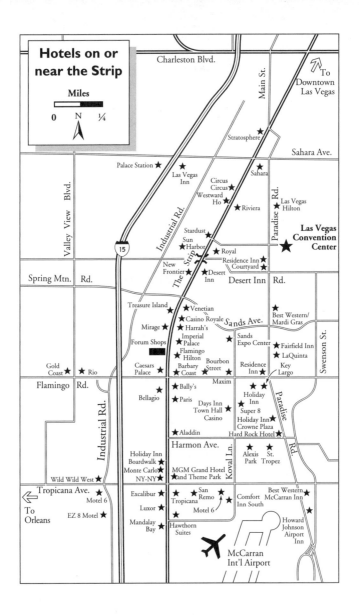

Hotels on or near the Strip

Miles

0   N   ¼

Charleston Blvd.

Main St.

To Downtown Las Vegas

Sahara Ave.

Palace Station ★

Las Vegas Inn ★

Stratosphere ★

Circus Circus ★

Sahara ★

Westward Ho ★

Riviera ★

Las Vegas Hilton ★

Paradise Rd.

Las Vegas Convention Center ★

Industrial Rd.

The Strip

15

Valley View Blvd.

Stardust ★

Sun Harbor ★

Royal ★

Residence Inn ★

Courtyard ★

New Frontier ★

Desert Inn ★

Desert Inn Rd.

Spring Mtn.   Rd.

Treasure Island ★

Venetian ★

Casino Royale ★

Sands Ave.

Best Western/ Mardi Gras ★

Swenson St.

Mirage ★

Harrah's ★

Imperial Palace ★

Sands Expo Center ★

Fairfield Inn ★

LaQuinta ★

Forum Shops

Flamingo Hilton ★

Bourbon Street

Residence Inn ★

Key Largo ★

Gold Coast ★

★ Rio

Caesars Palace ★

Barbary Coast ★

Flamingo   Rd.

Maxim ★

Bally's ★

Holiday Inn ★ ★

Paradise Rd.

Bellagio ★

Paris ★

Days Inn ★

Super 8 ★

Industrial Rd.

Town Hall Casino ★

Holiday Inn ★

Crowne Plaza

Aladdin ★

Hard Rock Hotel ★

Harmon Ave.

Koval Ln.

Alexis Park ★

St. Tropez ★

Holiday Inn Boardwalk ★

Monte Carlo ★

Wild Wild West ★

NY-NY ★

MGM Grand Hotel and Theme Park ★

Tropicana Ave. ★

Motel 6

To Orleans

Excalibur ★

Luxor ★

EZ 8 Motel ★

San Remo ★

Tropicana ★

Motel 6 ★

Comfort Inn South ★

Best Western ★

McCarran Inn ★

Howard Johnson Airport Inn ★

Mandalay Bay ★

Hawthorn Suites

McCarran Int'l Airport

streets intersecting Las Vegas Boulevard, and properties immediately west of the Strip (far side of I-15).

The Strip vs. Downtown for Leisure Travelers

Although there are excellent hotels on the Boulder Highway and elsewhere, most vacationers stay downtown or on/near the Strip. Downtown offers a good range of hotels, restaurants, and gambling, but only limited entertainment and fewer amenities such as swimming pools. By car, the Strip is 8 to 15 minutes from downtown via I-15. If you don't have a car, public transportation to the Strip is affordable and as efficient as traffic allows.

If you stay on the Strip, you're more likely to need a car or other transportation. Hotels are spread out and often pricier than downtown. Entertainment is varied and extensive, and recreational facilities rival the world's best.

Downtown is a multicultural melting pot with an adventurous, raw, robust feel. Everything seems intense and concentrated, a blur of action and light.

Although downtown caters to every class of clientele, it's less formal and generally a working man's venue. The Strip runs the gamut but tends to attract more high rollers, suburbanites, and business travelers.

If You Visit Las Vegas on Business

If you're going to Las Vegas for a trade show or convention, lodge as near as possible to the meeting site, ideally within walking distance. Many Strip hotel-casinos are convenient to citywide shows and conventions at the Las Vegas Convention Center and have good track records with business travelers.

Our maps will help you pinpoint lodging near your meeting site.

Citywide conventions often provide shuttles between major hotels and the Convention Center, and cabs are also available.

Large Hotel-Casinos vs. Small Hotels and Motels

If your itinerary calls for a car and a lot of coming and going, big hotels can be a pain. At the Luxor, Excalibur, and Las Vegas Hilton, for example, it can take 15 minutes to reach your room from your car if you self-park. If you plan to use the car frequently, stay in a smaller lodging with convenient parking.

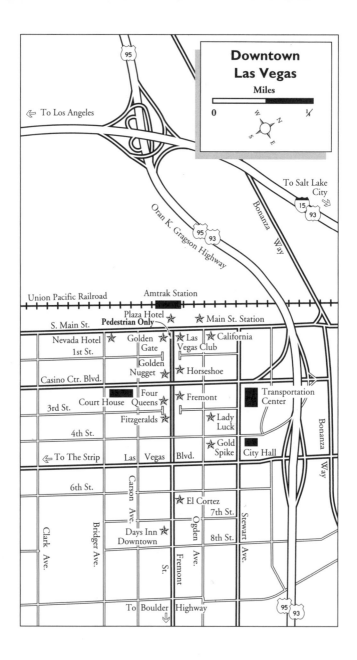

Downtown
Las Vegas

Miles

0

To Los Angeles

To Salt Lake City

Oran K. Gragson Highway

Bonanza Way

Union Pacific Railroad

Amtrak Station

S. Main St.

Plaza Hotel ⭐

Pedestrian Only

⭐ Main St. Station

Nevada Hotel

1st St.

⭐ Golden Gate ⭐

⭐ Las Vegas Club

⭐ California

Casino Ctr. Blvd.

Golden Nugget ⭐

⭐ Horseshoe

3rd St.

Court House

Four Queens ⭐

⭐ Fremont

Transportation Center

Fitzgeralds ⭐

⭐ Lady Luck

4th St.

To The Strip

Las Vegas Blvd.

⭐ Gold Spike

City Hall

Bonanza Way

6th St.

Carson Ave.

⭐ El Cortez

7th St.

Stewart Ave.

Clark Ave.

Bridger Ave.

Days Inn Downtown ⭐

Ogden Ave.

8th St.

Fremont St.

To Boulder Highway

Many visitors object to passing through a noisy, round-the-clock casino to reach their room. Staying at smaller properties without a casino eliminates this problem.

More comfortable or luxurious rooms aren't a certainty at large hotels. Any lodging can be threadbare or poorly designed. A large hotel, however, usually ensures superior amenities.

If you plan to tour mostly on foot or are attending a convention, a large hotel in a good location has the edge. If you want to immerse yourself in the atmosphere of Las Vegas, book a large hotel.

Getting Around: Location and Convenience

LAS VEGAS LODGING CONVENIENCE CHART

The following chart indicates how convenient a sampling of lodgings are to common destinations. Times are conservative.

Commuting Time in Minutes					
From:	**To:**				UNLV Thomas
Hotel	Las Vegas Strip	Convention Center	Down-town	McCarran Airport	& Mack Center
Aladdin	on Strip	8/cab	15/cab	7/cab	8/cab
Alexis Park	5/cab	8/cab	15/cab	5/cab	6/cab
Bally's	on Strip	8/cab	15/cab	7/cab	7/cab
Bellagio	on Strip	12/cab	15/cab	11/cab	12/cab
Best Western	6/cab	9/cab	15/cab	4/cab	7/cab
Bourbon Street	4/walk	8/cab	15/cab	7/cab	7/cab
Caesars Palace	on Strip	10/cab	12/cab	10/cab	10/cab
California	13/cab	15/cab	downtown	19/cab	19/cab
Circus Circus	on Strip	5/cab	13/cab	14/cab	13/cab
Comfort Inn	3/cab	9/cab	15/cab	4/cab	6/cab
Courtyard	4/cab	5/walk	15/cab	9/cab	8/cab
Desert Inn	on Strip	5/cab	15/cab	9/cab	9/cab
El Cortez	11/cab	15/cab	6/walk	16/cab	17/cab
Excalibur	on Strip	13/cab	14/cab	7/cab	8/cab
E-Z 8 Motel	4/cab	9/cab	12/cab	9/cab	10/cab

Commuting Time in Minutes (continued)

From: Hotel	To: Las Vegas Strip	Convention Center	Down-town	McCarran Airport	UNLV Thomas & Mack Center
Fiesta Hotel	18/cab	18/cab	10/cab	22/cab	22/cab
Fitzgeralds	14/cab	15/cab	downtown	17/cab	17/cab
Flamingo Hilton	on Strip	9/cab	13/cab	8/cab	8/cab
Four Queens	15/cab	15/cab	downtown	19/cab	17/cab
Four Seasons	on Strip	14/cab	16/cab	7/cab	13/cab
Fremont	15/cab	15/cab	downtown	19/cab	17/cab
Golden Nugget	14/cab	15/cab	downtown	18/cab	19/cab
Hard Rock Hotel	4/cab	6/cab	15/cab	6/cab	6/cab
Harrah's	on Strip	9/cab	15/cab	10/cab	10/cab
Holiday Inn Crowne Plaza	5/cab	5/cab	14/cab	8/cab	6/cab
Horseshoe	14/cab	15/cab	downtown	19/cab	19/cab
Howard Johnson	4/cab	14/cab	14/cab	9/cab	11/cab
Imperial Palace	on Strip	9/cab	15/cab	10/cab	10/cab
Lady Luck	14/cab	15/cab	3/walk	19/cab	18/cab
Las Vegas Hilton	5/cab	5/walk	13/cab	10/cab	8/cab
Luxor	on Strip	13/cab	15/cab	8/cab	10/cab
Mandalay Bay	on Strip	14/cab	16/cab	7/cab	13/cab
MGM Grand	on Strip	12/cab	15/cab	9/cab	9/cab
Mirage	on Strip	11/cab	15/cab	11/cab	10/cab
Monte Carlo	on Strip	12/cab	15/cab	11/cab	12/cab
New York–New York	on Strip	12/cab	15/cab	11/cab	12/cab
Palace Station	5/cab	10/cab	10/cab	14/cab	15/cab
Paris	on Strip	9/cab	15/cab	8/cab	8/cab
Rio	5/cab	14/cab	13/cab	10/cab	10/cab
Riviera	on Strip	4/cab	14/cab	11/cab	10/cab
Sahara	on Strip	4/cab	13/cab	13/cab	11/cab
St. Tropez	5/cab	6/cab	15/cab	7/cab	6/cab
Sam's Town	20/cab	25/cab	20/cab	18/cab	17/cab

Commuting Time in Minutes (continued)					
From:	**To:**				UNLV Thomas
Hotel	Las Vegas Strip	Convention Center	Down-town	McCarran Airport	& Mack Center
Santa Fe	27/cab	30/cab	23/cab	33/cab	36/cab
Showboat	19/cab	18/cab	12/cab	21/cab	20/cab
Stardust	on Strip	4/cab	13/cab	12/cab	10/cab
Stratosphere	3/cab	7/cab	9/cab	14/cab	14/cab
Sunset Station	18/cab	17/cab	18/cab	16/cab	15/cab
Treasure Island	on Strip	11/cab	14/cab	11/cab	10/cab
Tropicana	on Strip	11/cab	15/cab	6/cab	9/cab
Vacation Village	8/cab	18/cab	18/cab	8/cab	12/cab
Venetian	on Strip	9/cab	14/cab	8/cab	8/cab

Commuting to Downtown from the Strip

From the Strip, access I-15 at Tropicana Avenue, Flamingo Road, Spring Mountain Road, or Sahara Avenue. Northbound on I-15, keep right and follow signs for downtown and US 95 South. Exit onto Casino Center Boulevard, and you'll be in the middle of downtown convenient to several parking garages. Driving time varies between about 14 minutes from the south end of the Strip (I-15 via Tropicana Avenue) to about 6 minutes from the north end (I-15 via Sahara Avenue).

Commuting to the Strip from Downtown

From downtown, pick up US 95 (and then I-15) by going north on either Fourth Street or Las Vegas Boulevard. Driving time is 6–14 minutes, depending on your destination.

Free Connections

Traffic on the Strip is so awful that hotels are creating new alternatives for getting around.

1. A monorail connects Bally's, Paris Las Vegas, and MGM Grand on the east side of the Strip, while an elevated tram links Bellagio and Monte Carlo on the west side. Farther south on the west side, a shuttle serves Excalibur, Luxor, Mandalay Bay, and Four Seasons.

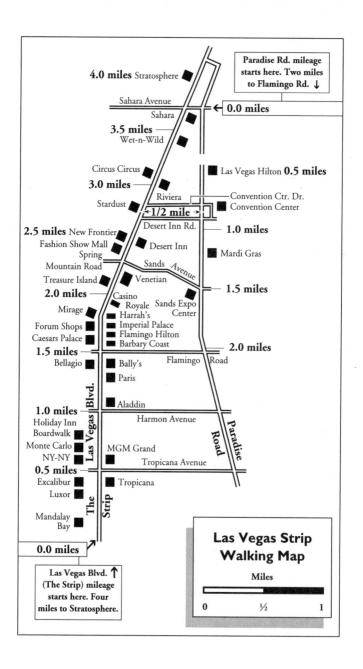

4.0 miles Stratosphere

Sahara Avenue

Sahara

← **0.0 miles**

Paradise Rd. mileage starts here. Two miles to Flamingo Rd. ↓

3.5 miles
Wet-n-Wild

Circus Circus
3.0 miles

■ Las Vegas Hilton **0.5 miles**

Riviera

Convention Ctr. Dr.
Convention Center

Stardust
←**1/2 mile**→

Desert Inn Rd.

2.5 miles New Frontier
Fashion Show Mall
Spring
Mountain Road
Treasure Island
2.0 miles

Desert Inn

1.0 miles

■ Mardi Gras

Sands Avenue

Venetian

1.5 miles

Sands Expo Center

Casino
Royale
Mirage
Harrah's
Forum Shops
Imperial Palace
Caesars Palace
Flamingo Hilton
1.5 miles
Barbary Coast

2.0 miles

Bellagio

Bally's

Flamingo Road

Paris

Las Vegas Blvd.

1.0 miles
Holiday Inn
Boardwalk
Monte Carlo
NY-NY
0.5 miles

Aladdin

Harmon Avenue

MGM Grand

Tropicana Avenue

Paradise Road

Excalibur
Luxor

Tropicana

The Strip

Mandalay
Bay

0.0 miles ↗

Las Vegas Blvd. ↑ (The Strip) mileage starts here. Four miles to Stratosphere.

Las Vegas Strip Walking Map

Miles

0   ½   1

2. A new, free express-shuttle operates just north of Holiday Inn Boardwalk to the Golden Nugget downtown. Buses depart on the hour from noon until 11 p.m. To return to the Strip, validate your boarding ticket at the Golden Nugget, then catch the return shuttle, departing on the half-hour from 1:30 p.m. until 12:30 a.m. You can only make a round-trip from the Strip to the Golden Nugget and back to the Strip; you can't initiate a round-trip from downtown.

3. The Rio operates a shuttle from the Rio Visitor's Center to the Rio. Shuttles also link Barbary Coast on the northeast corner of the Strip and Flamingo to the Gold Coast about a mile west.

4. Free shuttle service from the Polo Towers near Aladdin to the Stratosphere runs on the hour northbound to the Stratosphere and on the half-hour for southbound returns from 9 a.m. until 11 p.m.

What's in an Address?

DOWNTOWN

The heart of the downtown casino area is Fremont Street between Fourth Street (on the east) and Main Street (on the west). Hotel-casinos on this quarter-mile called Glitter Gulch include the Plaza Hotel, Golden Gate, Las Vegas Club, Binion's Horseshoe, Golden Nugget, Sam Boyd's Fremont, Four Queens, and Fitzgeralds. Parallel to Fremont and one block north on Ogden Avenue are the California, Lady Luck, and the Gold Spike. Main Street Station is on Main Street at the Ogden intersection.

Although hotel quality and price vary greatly downtown, all properties are convenient to the action. The exception is El Cortez, three blocks east.

THE STRIP

Location is of paramount importance on the Strip.

Some promotional photographs make the Strip look compact. But the Strip is about seven miles long, running from southwest of the airport to downtown. Only the four miles between Mandalay Bay and the Stratosphere contain the large casinos and other visitor attractions.

The Best Locations on the Strip

Beware of hotels and motels claiming to be on the Strip but not located between Mandalay Bay and the Stratosphere. Their location will disappoint you.

Some Strip sections are preferable. The south anchor Mandalay Bay is a quarter-mile from Luxor, its closest neighbor. The Stratosphere and the Sahara are somewhat isolated at the other end. In between are distinct clusters of hotels and casinos.

Strip Cluster 1: The Cluster of the Giants   At the intersection of the Strip and Tropicana Avenue are three of the world's largest hotels. The MGM Grand Hotel is the largest U.S. hotel. Diagonally across from the MGM Grand is Excalibur, the third-largest hotel in the United States. The other two corners are occupied by New York–New York and the Tropicana. Nearby to the south is Luxor (second largest), and north are the Holiday Inn Boardwalk and Monte Carlo. The San Remo is on Tropicana across from the MGM Grand. From the intersection of the Strip and Tropicana, it's a half-mile south to Mandalay Bay and a three-tenths-mile hike north to the Aladdin. The next cluster of major hotels and casinos is one mile north at Flamingo Road.

Strip Cluster 2: The Grand Cluster   From Flamingo Road to Spring Mountain Road (also called Sands Avenue, and farther east, Twain Avenue) lies the greatest numerical concentration of major hotels and casinos. If you want to stay on the Strip and walk wherever you go, this is the best location. At Flamingo Road and Las Vegas Boulevard are Bally's, Caesars Palace, Barbary Coast, Paris, and Bellagio. East on Flamingo are Bourbon Street and Maxim. Toward town are the Flamingo, O'Shea's, Imperial Palace, Mirage, Harrah's, Casino Royale, the Venetian, and Treasure Island. Also in this cluster are the outstanding Forum Shops and Grand Canal Shoppes. You could stay a week in this cluster (without getting into a car) and not run out of interesting sights, good restaurants, and entertainment. But traffic at the intersection of the Strip and Flamingo Road is the city's worst.

Strip Cluster 3   Easy access distinguishes another nice section of the Strip, from Spring Mountain Road to the New Frontier and

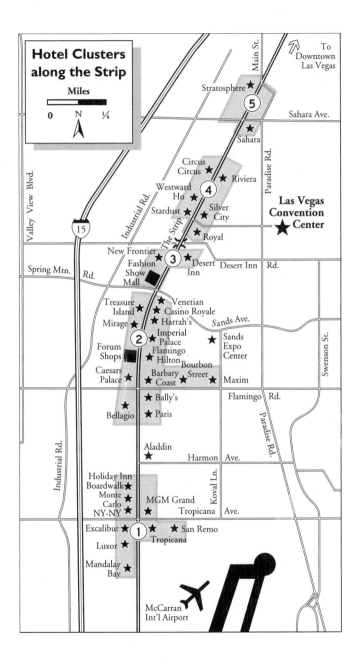

Hotel Clusters along the Strip

Miles

0   N   ¼

To Downtown Las Vegas

Main St.

Stratosphere ★
⑤

Sahara Ave.

Sahara ★

Circus Circus ★   ★ Riviera

Westward Ho ★   ④

Stardust ★   ★ Silver City

Paradise Rd.

Las Vegas Convention ★ Center

★ Royal

New Frontier ★
③
Fashion Show Mall   Desert Inn   Desert Inn Rd.

Spring Mtn. Rd.

Treasure Island ★   ★ Venetian
★ Casino Royale
Mirage ★   ★ Harrah's

Sands Ave.

②   Imperial ★ Palace

Forum Shops   Flamingo ★   Sands Expo Center
★ Hilton   Bourbon Street

Caesars Palace ★   Barbary ★ Coast   Maxim ★

Swenson St.

★ Bally's   Flamingo Rd.

Bellagio ★   ★ Paris

Paradise Rd.

Aladdin ★   Harmon Ave.

Industrial Rd.

Holiday Inn Boardwalk ★
Monte Carlo ★   MGM Grand
NY-NY ★   ★   Tropicana Ave.

Koval Ln.

Excalibur ★ ① ★★   ★ San Remo
Tropicana
Luxor ★

Mandalay Bay ★

McCarran Int'l Airport

Valley View Blvd.

Industrial Rd.

15

The Strip

33

the Desert Inn. The Desert Inn and the New Frontier (across the street) can be reached by either of two roads. This cluster is perfect for visitors who prefer a major Strip hotel but want to avoid traffic. Although the Desert Inn and the New Frontier are about a quarter-mile from the nearest casinos in either direction, both are within a four-minute walk of the excellent Fashion Show Mall. This cluster is four minutes by cab or a 16-minute walk from the convention center.

Strip Cluster 4   The third-largest cluster of major hotels lies on the half-mile between Convention Center Drive and Riviera Boulevard. Here, near the convention center, are the Stardust, Westward Ho, Slots of Fun, Silver City, Royal Hotel, Riviera, and Circus Circus. Less upscale than hotels and casinos in the "grand cluster," they're nonetheless great for people-watching and offer acceptable dining and entertainment. Traffic in this cluster is woefully congested.

Strip Cluster 5   The relatively isolated cluster near the intersection of Las Vegas Boulevard and Sahara Avenue contains Wet 'n Wild water theme park, the Sahara, and, about a third-mile toward town, the Stratosphere. Visitors with cars are convenient to the Strip, the Convention Center, and downtown.

Just Off the Strip

If you have a car and being on the Strip isn't a big deal to you, excellent hotel-casinos are on Paradise Road and east and west of the Strip on intersecting roads.

Boulder Highway, Green Valley, and North Las Vegas

Twenty minutes from the Strip in North Las Vegas are Texas Station, the Fiesta, and, at the edge of civilization, the Santa Fe. All have good restaurants, comfortable rooms, and lively themes. On the Boulder Highway southeast of town are Showboat, Sam's Town, and Nevada Palace. Also southeast are Sunset Station and the Reserve in Green Valley. These areas cater primarily to locals. The posh, new Resort at Summerlin is northwest of town.

Sneak Routes

Traffic clogs the heart of the Strip at many hours. Fortunately, most large hotels have back entrances on less-trafficked roads. In-

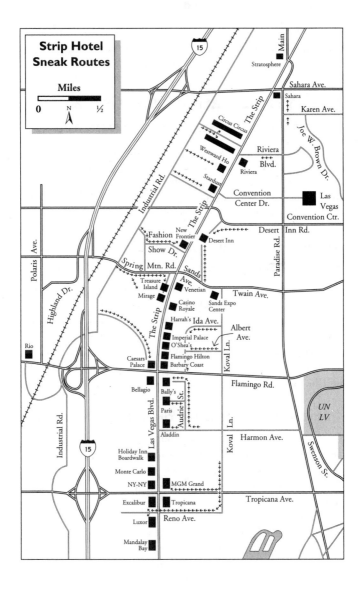

Strip Hotel Sneak Routes

Miles

0   N   ½

15

Main

Stratosphere

Sahara Ave.

Sahara

Karen Ave.

Joe W. Brown Dr.

Circus Circus

The Strip

Riviera
Blvd.

Westward Ho

Riviera

Stardust

Convention
Center Dr.

Las
Vegas
Convention Ctr.

Industrial Rd.

The Strip

Desert Inn Rd.

Fashion
Show Dr.

New
Frontier

Desert Inn

Paradise Rd.

Polaris Ave.

Spring Mtn. Rd.

Sands
Ave.

Treasure
Island

Venetian

Twain Ave.

Highland Dr.

Mirage

Casino
Royale

Sands Expo
Center

The Strip

Harrah's

Ida Ave.

Albert
Ave.

Imperial Palace

Rio

O'Shea's

Koval Ln.

Caesars
Palace

Flamingo Hilton

Barbary Coast

Bellagio

Bally's

Flamingo Rd.

Paris

Audrie St.

Las Vegas Blvd.

Koval Ln.

UN
LV

Aladdin

Harmon Ave.

Industrial Rd.

Holiday Inn
Boardwalk

Swenson St.

15

Monte Carlo

NY-NY

MGM Grand

Excalibur

Tropicana

Tropicana Ave.

Luxor

Reno Ave.

Mandalay
Bay

dustrial Road and I-15 parallel the Strip on the west, providing access to hotels on the west side of Las Vegas Boulevard. Paradise Road and Koval Lane do the same for the east side.

Room Reservations: Getting a Good Room, Getting a Good Deal

Because Las Vegas is popular for short getaways, weekend occupancy averages an astounding 92% of capacity for hotels and 70% for motels. Weekday occupancy for hotels is a respectable 83%; for motels, 63%. This means: Don't leave home without reservations, especially if major events pack the city.

THE WACKY WORLD OF LAS VEGAS HOTEL RESERVATIONS

Rooms generally are administered by different departments: the casino (for high rollers), the front desk (general public), independent wholesalers (group or individual travel packages), sales and marketing (special events), and national reservations systems. This means the front desk may tell you the hotel is sold out, but a call a few days later may find that rooms unsold by another department are available.

GETTING THE BEST DEAL ON A ROOM

Compared to lodging elsewhere, rooms in Las Vegas are so inexpensive that cost-cutting strategies may seem gratuitous. If you are accustomed to paying $120 a night for a room, you can afford 70% of the hotels in town. If, however, you want top value for your dollar, read on.

Beating Rack Rates

The benchmark for making cost comparisons is the hotel's "rack rate," or standard rate. This nondiscounted price is what you would pay if, space available, you walked in off the street and rented a room. Assume that the rack rate is the most you should have to pay.

To learn the standard rate, call room reservations at hotels of your choice. Each type of room will have its own rate. Have the reservationist explain the differences among rooms.

The Season

In December, the town is empty except for National Finals Rodeo week in early December and Christmas/New Year's week. In January, the town is packed during the Consumer Electronics Show and Super Bowl weekend, and pretty much dead otherwise. During these months, most hotels offer amazing deals on lodging. Rates also may be reduced in July and August.

Sorting Out the Sellers and the Options

Given the many sources of rooms, it's almost impossible to find out who is offering the best deal.

Though it's only an approximation, here's a list of rates and packages available, ranked from the best to the worst value.

Room Rates and Packages	Sold or Administered by
1. Gambler's rate	Casino or hotel
2. December, January, and summer specials	Hotel reservations or marketing department
3. Wholesaler packages	Independent wholesalers
4. Tour operator packages	Tour operators
5. Reservation service discounts	Independent wholesalers and consolidators
6. Half-price programs	Half-price program operators
7. Commercial airline packages	Commercial airlines
8. Hotel packages	Hotel sales and marketing
9. Corporate rate	Hotel reservations
10. Hotel standard room rate	Hotel reservations
11. Convention rate	Convention sponsor

Don't forget that if you get the gambler's rate, you'll be obligated to wager, and that could make it the most expensive option.

Taking Advantage of Special Deals

When you call, always ask the reservationist if the hotel has any packages or specials, including gaming specials if you plan to gamble. If the reservationist isn't knowledgeable, ask to be transferred to the sales and marketing staff, and question them.

If you have a lot of time before your trip, contact the hotel and ask about joining its slot club. Although only a few hotels will send you an application, inquiring will categorize you as a gambler on a hotel's mailing list. Once in Las Vegas, join the slot clubs of hotel-casinos you like. This ensures you'll be notified of specials you can use on subsequent visits.

Having shopped the hotel for deals, check tour operator and wholesaler packages advertised in your local newspaper, and compare them with those in the Sunday edition of the *Los Angeles Times*. Next, check packages offered by airline tour services; always ask reservationists if there are specials with any hotels.

Discuss the better deals and packages, regardless of source, with a travel agent. Explain which you favor and ask if he or she can do better. Review all options, then select the deal that best fits your schedule, requirements, and budget.

Timing Is Everything

If occupancy is high for a date, rates will be, too. But if many rooms are available, rates will be lower. This is true all year but especially in "off-peak" times.

At some hotels, a standard room costs 20% less if you check in Monday through Thursday (even though you may stay through the weekend). The rate on the same room with weekend check-in will be higher and may not change if you stay into the following week.

Picking a Travel Agent

When you call your travel agent, ask if he or she has been to Las Vegas. Firsthand experience means everything. If the answer is no, find another agent or be prepared to give your agent a lot of direction. Do not accept any recommendations at face value. Check the location and rates of any suggested hotel and make certain it suits your itinerary. Do the same for packages.

Packages in conjunction with airlines, including Delta's Vacations or American's Fly-Away Vacations, will probably be more expensive than those offered by high-volume wholesalers that work with several airlines.

No Room at the Inn (Maybe) If you're having trouble getting a reservation at the hotel of your choice, let your travel agent assist you. He or she might find a package with a wholesaler or tour operator that bypasses the hotel reservations department. Or, he or she can call the sales and marketing department of the hotel and ask them, as a favor, to find you a room.

No Room at the Inn (for Real) More frequently than you would imagine, Las Vegas hotels overbook their rooms. To protect yourself, always guarantee your first night with a credit card, send a deposit if required, and insist on a written confirmation of your reservation. Have your confirmation when you check in.

Precautions notwithstanding, the hotel still might have canceled your reservation. If you're told you have no room, demand that the hotel find you a room on the premises or at another convenient hotel (comparable room at the same or better rate). Should the desk clerk balk, demand to see the reservations manager. If the reservations manager stonewalls, go to the general manager. Do not leave until the issue has been resolved.

WHERE THE DEALS ARE

Tour Operators and Wholesalers

At lower-occupancy days or seasons, hotels allot rooms at considerable discounts to tour operators, travel brokers, travel wholesalers, and travel packagers who resell them for a profit. Sought-after weekend lodging also may be available.

Check the travel section of your Sunday paper for ads for packages or tours to Las Vegas. Book suitable packages directly by calling the phone number listed, or have your travel agent call.

If ads in your paper offer no worthwhile packages, go to a newsstand and buy a Sunday paper, preferably from Los Angeles but also from San Diego, Phoenix, Salt Lake City, Denver, or Chicago. These cities are hot markets for Las Vegas, and their newspapers almost always advertise packages.

Not all of a package may be available to you; air connections may be city-specific. But you may buy the "land only" part of the package. You get the discounted room and amenities (car, shows, etc.) but handle your own travel arrangements.

Half-Price Programs

Most half-price programs charge an annual membership fee or directory subscription charge of $25 to $125. On enrollment, you get a membership card and a directory listing participating hotels. There are many restrictions and exceptions. Also, the discount may be smaller than 50%.

The programs with the largest selection of hotels in Las Vegas are Encore, Travel America at Half Price (Entertainment Publications), International Travel Card, and Quest.

Deeply discounted rooms through half-price programs are not commissionable to travel agents. Thus, you generally must make your own inquiries and reservations.

Half-Price Programs	
Encore	(800) 638-0930
Entertainment Publications	(800) 285-5525
International Travel Card	(800) 342-0558
Quest	(800) 638-9819

Players Club

The most visible discount travel club selling Las Vegas is Players Club. The group advertises savings of 25–60% on lodging, cruises, shows, and dining (other destinations are included). Annual membership is $192 (plus $10 handling fee). Participating Las Vegas hotels are Bally's, San Remo, Flamingo Hilton, Las Vegas Hilton, Luxor, Holiday Inn Boardwalk, and Stardust.

A determined person who knows Las Vegas can probably beat Players Club's deal but will have to invest a lot of time for a package only marginally less expensive.

If you're interested in Players Club, call (800) 275-6600. An operator will take your name, address, and phone number. Tell the aggressive telemarketer who calls that you don't have time for the sales pitch, and insist that membership information be mailed to you. Membership cancellation is handled without hassle.

Reservation Services	
Hotel Reservations Network	(800) 96-HOTEL
City Wide Reservations	(800) 733-6644
RMC Travel Center	(800) 782-2674 or (800) 245-5738
Accommodations Express	(800) 444-7666

Reservation Services

Wholesalers and consolidators frequently represent themselves as "reservation services." When you call, you can ask for a rate quote for a particular hotel or for their best available deal in a specific area. If there's a maximum you're willing to pay, say so. Chances are, the service will find something that will work for you.

We've found reservation services more useful in finding rooms when they're scarce than in obtaining deep discounts.

Hotel-Sponsored Packages

In addition to selling rooms through tour operators, consolidators, and wholesalers, most hotels periodically offer exceptional deals of their own. Promotion of specials tends to be only in the hotels' primary markets. Look for these specials in Southern California newspapers, or call the hotel. Reservationists usually don't tell you of specials. *You have to ask.*

Exit Information Guide

Exit Information Guide publishes a free book of coupons for bargain rates at hotels throughout California and Nevada. For $3 ($5 Canadian), EIG will mail a copy (third class) before you make your reservations. Las Vegas properties listed in the guide are generally smaller, nongaming hotels. Contact:

Exit Information Guide
4205 NW Sixth St.
Gainesville, FL 32609
(352) 371-3948

For Business Travelers

CONVENTION RATES: HOW THE SYSTEM WORKS

Business travelers almost always pay more for their rooms than leisure travelers do.

For citywide conventions, huge numbers of rooms are blocked in hotels. Hotels negotiate a rate with the convention sponsor, who then sells the rooms itself. Since hotels prefer gamblers or leisure travelers to conventioneers (who usually have limited time to gamble), the negotiated price tends to be $10–50 per night above rack rate.

Strategies for Beating Convention Rates

To get around convention rates:

1. Buy a package from a tour operator or a wholesaler   You won't have to deal with the convention's reservations office or with a hotel's reservations department. Many packages allow you to buy extra days at a discount if the package dates don't coincide with your meeting.

If you beat the convention rate by booking a package or getting a room from a wholesaler, don't blow your cover when you check in. If you walk up to the registration desk in a business suit with a convention badge, the hotel will void your package and charge you the convention rate. Ditto, checkout.

2. Find a hotel that doesn't block rooms   Many downtown, North Las Vegas, and Boulder Highway hotels, as well as a few on the Strip, don't block rooms for conventions. Get a list of your convention's "official" hotels and match it against the hotels listed in this guide. Any hotel we list that isn't on the sponsor's list is not blocking rooms for your convention. This means you can deal with the nonparticipating hotels directly and get their regular rate.

3. Reserve late   Thirty to sixty days before a citywide convention or show, the front desk reservations staff in a given hotel will take over management of blocked rooms. "Room Res," in conjunction with the general manager, is responsible for ensuring the hotel runs at capacity during the event. If blocked rooms aren't being booked as expected, the manager may lower the price for attendees. A convention-goer who books a room at the last minute might obtain a rate lower than did attendees who booked early through the sponsor.

THE LAS VEGAS CONVENTION CENTER

The Las Vegas Convention Center is the nation's second-largest convention and trade-show facility. Much of its 1.6 million square feet of exhibit space is in one building. Divided into seven halls, the building houses the largest single-floor exhibit area in North America.

The complex has a new lobby and public areas, a kitchen that can cater a banquet for 12,000 people, and 89 meeting rooms. One million square feet of additional exhibit space will come on-line in spring 2000. Serving as headquarters for shows and conventions drawing as many as 250,000 delegates, the Convention Center is on Paradise Road, one block off the Strip and three miles from the airport.

The Las Vegas Convention and Visitors Authority also operates Cashman Field Center, home of Las Vegas's AAA baseball team. The center contains a 2,000-seat theater and 100,000 square feet of meeting and exhibit space. For information, call (702) 892-0711.

Lodging Nearest the Las Vegas Convention Center

While convention-goers lodge all over town, a few hotels are within walking distance of the Convention Center.

Next door is the Las Vegas Hilton, with more than 3,100 rooms. The hotel routinely is headquarters for Convention Center events and offers an additional 220,000 square feet of exhibit, ballroom, banquet, special event, and meeting space. The Convention Center is a five-minute walk from the Hilton's lobby.

A long half-block away (to its rear entrance) is the 2,075-room Riviera Hotel. Like the Hilton, the Riviera is often headquarters for large Convention Center events and offers supplemental space. The walk from the Riviera's rear (eastern) entrance to the Convention Center is about ten minutes.

Parking at the Las Vegas Convention Center

About one-third of the 7,000 available spaces are in front of the complex, off Paradise Road. The remainder are off East Desert

Hotels within a 20-Minute Walk of the Convention Center		
Amerisuites	202 suites	7-minute walk
Circus Circus	3,741 rooms	15-minute walk
Desert Inn	715 rooms	18-minute walk
La Concha	352 rooms	15-minute walk
Las Vegas Courtyard	149 rooms	6-minute walk
Las Vegas Hilton	3,174 rooms	5-minute walk
Mardi Gras Inn	314 suites	12-minute walk
Marriott Suites	255 suites	9-minute walk
New Frontier	988 rooms	20-minute walk
Residence Inn	192 suites	7-minute walk
Riviera	2,075 rooms	10-minute walk
Royal Hotel	220 rooms	12-minute walk
Stardust	2,500 rooms	15-minute walk

Inn Road. The front lot is usually packed. Lots off East Desert Inn Road usually have space available.

Attendees are often required to enter through the Convention Center's main entrance. In this case, convention-goers using the East Desert Inn parking lots must hike around the south side of the complex to the front door, a seven- to ten-minute walk. Or, attendees with badges may enter through the doors on the complex's south side.

Cabs and Shuttles to the Convention Center

Citywide conventions often provide complimentary bus service from major hotels. If you're staying at a smaller hotel, walk to the nearest large hotel on the route. Cabs can be scarce at events' daily opening and closing times. City buses ($1.50) and the Las Vegas Strip Trolley ($1.40) also are available from larger hotels. Exact fare is required.

Generally, a car is less hassle than cabs and shuttles.

Comfort Zones: Matching Guests with Hotels

Each Las Vegas property targets a carefully defined audience. This effort to please a specific population of guests creates what we call a "comfort zone." If you're in the group a hotel strives to please, you'll feel comfortable and will have much in common with other guests. If you fail to determine the comfort zone before you go, you may choose a hotel you won't enjoy.

Hotel descriptions on subsequent pages detail the atmosphere and clientele of the city's major lodgings.

Democracy in the Casinos

Hotels and casinos continue to be characterized as appealing to "high rollers" (wealthy visitors who gamble in earnest) or "grinds" (less affluent, nickel-and-dime bettors), but the distinction is increasingly blurred. For many years, the slot machine was symbolic of the grinds. Unable to join high-stakes "table games," blue-collar gamblers sat for hours pumping the arms of slots. More recently, however, slot machines' popularity among all gamblers has democratized casinos. The silver-haired lady at the quarter slots is now viewed as a highly valuable customer, and casinos forgo the impression of exclusivity in order to make her comfortable. After all, slots now contribute 40%–100% of a casino's bottom line.

Hotels with Casinos

How to Avoid Reading the Hotel-Casino Descriptions   If you don't care how a place "feels" and want just the facts, skip to the Hotel Information Chart at the back of the book.

Aladdin

The Aladdin, closed since November 1997, will be replaced in early 2000 with a vastly enlarged hotel-casino complex. The new 2,600-room Aladdin will sport a desert kingdom theme and feature a huge retail, dining, and entertainment complex.

Arizona Charlie's

Patronized primarily by locals, Arizona Charlie's is a working person's casino with southwestern ranch flavor. Everything is informal. And it's busy, with lots of slots, some table games, a sports book*, burgers and beer, and a lounge featuring medium-name entertainment. Improvements include some very nice guest rooms.

Bally's

A complete resort, Bally's is blessed with exceptional restaurants, one of Las Vegas's better buffets, and *the* best Sunday champagne brunch. Entertainment is top quality. Guest rooms are large and comfortable, and the hotel is easy to navigate. The casino is immense, open, and elegantly modern.

Bally's caters to meetings and conventions; you won't feel out of place in a business suit. Guests usually are younger than 40, many from Southern California, Chicago, and elsewhere in the Midwest. Bally's also has a loyal Spanish-speaking clientele.

Barbary Coast

The Barbary Coast is an old-fashioned casino for real gamblers. Table games reign supreme. The gourmet restaurant, Michael's, is regarded by many locals as the city's most dependable. There is no showroom or swimming pool, and most rooms are reserved for regular customers.

Bellagio

Steve Wynn established a new standard for Las Vegas hotel-casinos when he opened the Mirage in 1989. Now, with Bellagio he's bumping up the standard: he intends it to be the world's best hotel.

With its main entrance off the Strip just south of Flamingo Road, Bellagio is inspired by a northern Italian village. The facade is reminiscent of the themed architecture he employed at Treasure Island. The Bellagio village is arrayed along the west and north sides of a man-made lake, where dancing fountains provide a spectacle more dignified than the Mirage's volcano or Treasure Island's buccaneer battle. Surprisingly, the Italian village theme of Bellagio's lakefront facade is largely abandoned in the interior. The vast spaces are exceedingly tasteful and unquestionably sophisticated and lovely, yet they fail to evoke the fun, whimsy, and curiosity so intrinsic to the Mirage and Treasure Island.

---

*A sports book is a casino facility, sometimes simple, often elaborate, where wagers are taken on sporting events.

The 3,000-room hotel, casino, dining, and shopping complex aims to become Las Vegas's prestige address. Imported marble and European antiques are used throughout. Restaurants have panoramic views. In the showroom is the new *Cirque du Soleil "O"* production. The Bellagio Gallery of Fine Art features works by the world's masters. And Bellagio serves one of Las Vegas's best—and not unexpectedly one of the city's most expensive—buffets.

Rates for guest rooms and suites are among the Strip's highest, and the hotel's target market is said to include high rollers and discriminating business travelers. The Bellagio is a friendly place to stay and gamble and not at all pretentious.

Boardwalk Holiday Inn

The Boardwalk is a modest hotel-casino blessed with a good location. Acquired in 1994 by Holiday Inn, the property has been rebuilt with a Coney Island–boardwalk theme. All table games are represented, but slots are emphasized. Dining is limited to counter service, a buffet, and a small coffee shop. The only entrance is from the Strip, complicating auto access. Owing to the Holiday Inn connection, guests run the gamut.

Boulder Station

Boulder Station is a clone of Palace Station, sharing its railroad theme and emphasis on good food and lounge entertainment. The tasteful casino includes one of Las Vegas's nicest sports books. Like its sister property, Boulder Station is an oasis for the hungry, with a great buffet, several good full-service restaurants, and possibly the best fast food in any casino. The 300 guest rooms are modest but comfortable. Clientele is primarily locals and Southern Californians.

We prefer the casino at Boulder Station and the guest rooms at Palace Station. Boulder Station is much less crowded and much easier to access by car.

Caesars Palace

Of Las Vegas's theme hotels and casinos, Caesars Palace was the first to fully realize its potential. Its Roman theme has been executed with astounding artistry and detail. Incredibly, the vaulted ceilings, classic statuary, and graceful arches accommodate the clanking of coins and activity of the pits.

Caesars Palace provides two luxurious casinos, excellent restaurants, beautiful landscaping, top entertainment, exquisite guest rooms, and all of the amenities of a world-class resort. Also featured is Caesars Magical Empire, a dining and entertainment complex. The adjoining Forum Shops is one of the nation's most extraordinary themed-shopping complexes.

Guest rooms in the new, 29-floor tower offer some of the Strip's best views (floors five and up). Outside is an elaborate new "Roman bath" swimming complex. For the less energetic are the IMAX theater and the 3D simulator *Race for Atlantis.*

Designed for high rollers, Caesars has a broad range of clientele from the East, Midwest, and Southern California and is popular with Asians and Hispanics. We find Caesars friendly and easygoing, though pricey. As a tourist attraction, it's a must.

California

The California is a pleasant downtown hotel-casino with excellent, moderately priced restaurants and a largely Hawaiian and Filipino clientele. The casino rambles but is short on elbowroom. Some properties are happenings; the California is simply a mellow place to stay or gamble.

Casino Royale

Across from the Mirage, the Casino Royale has about 150 guest rooms. Small, accessible, and unpretentious, it provides bargain lodging in the Strip's high-rent district. The casino is crowded and slot-heavy. Clientele ranges from tour groups to convention-goers on a budget, to folks who couldn't get rooms elsewhere on the block.

Circus Circus

Circus Circus was the first hotel on the Strip to pursue the family trade. Children, young adults, retirees, and novice or modest gamblers feel welcome. Dollar blackjack and nickel slots abound in the noisy casino. The circus theme, both exciting and wholesome, is ubiquitous. Top-quality circus acts perform (free).

The complex has a very good steakhouse, an inexpensive buffet, an RV park, and a monorail. Circus Circus was the first casino to establish a nonsmoking gaming area. Adventuredome, a desert canyon–themed amusement park, occupies a giant pink dome (see page 148). A new hotel tower and restaurant arcade adjoin it.

Desert Inn

The Desert Inn is possibly the city's most complete resort. It has the area's best golf course plus tennis, an exceptional pool, and a complete spa. Elegant and understated, without any theme, the Desert Inn has nothing to prove. Its tasteful guest rooms, fine restaurants, celebrity/production showroom, and chandeliered casino make it the self-confident aristocrat in Las Vegas's sea of excess.

It's expensive but still an exceptional value. Self-parking is close and convenient. Guests tend to be professionals, business travelers, and sportsmen. Popular with Southern Californians and southwesterners, the Desert Inn also draws Latin Americans and Asians.

El Cortez

El Cortez, east of downtown, caters to seniors, motor-coach tours, and blue-collar locals. The rambling casino—the city's oldest original (1941)—is congested; slots are the major draw. Food and drink are bargains, and loose slots give a lot of play for patrons' money. Guest rooms are quite nice and an exceptional value.

Excalibur

The Excalibur pursues upscale families. By combining a Knights of the Round Table theme, restaurants with giant portions, family-oriented entertainment, and moderate cost, the Excalibur "packs 'em in," especially on weekends. A Las Vegas rendition of a medieval realm, the Excalibur is oversized and garish.

Restaurants and shops are integrated into a medieval village on the top of three floors. On the lower floor are an arcade of midway games, the showroom (jousting tournaments are featured), and a movie/ride simulating a roller coaster. The middle level contains the casino, a roomy and festive place with '50s decor.

The Excalibur is the nation's third-largest hotel (behind the MGM Grand and Luxor), and it certainly has the world's largest hotel parking lot. (Trams haul in the patrons.) If you can see beyond the crowds, parking-lot commute, plastic medieval theme, and guest rooms with showers but no tubs, there's value. Food and entertainment are good and priced right.

Fiesta

The Mexican-themed Fiesta was the first of several casinos at the intersection of Rancho Drive and Lake Mead Boulevard in North

Las Vegas. It has 100 guest rooms, a slot-packed casino, a food court, and a country dance hall. Mexican and southwestern restaurants are the major draw. On Sunday is a good Margarita Brunch. The Fiesta draws locals.

Fitzgeralds

Fitzgeralds anchors the east end of Glitter Gulch downtown. The casino is large and compartmentalized. Renovation largely scuttled Fitzgeralds "Luck of the Irish" theme, sacrificing warmth and coziness. Upper-floor rooms afford fine views, and corner rooms with hot tubs are a great bargain. Guests tend to be older travelers and midwestern retirees. Gamblers are a mix of regulars and bargain hunters lured by visitor-guide ads for free gifts.

Flamingo Hilton

Built with mob money in the '40s and acquired by the Hilton chain in 1970, the Flamingo blends Las Vegas hyperbole and corporate pragmatism. It was the Strip's first super-resort. Today, with its 3,642 rooms, four towers, and prime location, it's the centerpiece of the Strip's most prestigious block.

Hilton transformed the Flamingo into a very dependable chain hotel. Flashier than its sister properties, the Las Vegas Hilton and Bally's, the Flamingo is also less formal, attracting leisure and business travelers from many states plus Japan. The bustling casino retains the hotel's signature Miami pinks, magentas, and tangerines and includes a sports book. Restaurants are consistent and the buffet passable. Bonuses are a fine production show and creative lounge entertainment.

Four Queens

The Four Queens downtown offers good food, renovated guest rooms, and a positively cheery casino. Glistening, light decor enhanced by tropical-print carpet makes the casino feel fun, upbeat, and clean. Hotel guests tend to be middle-aged or older and come from Southern California, Texas, Hawaii, and the Midwest. Locals love Hugo's Cellar restaurant.

Four Seasons

An exclusive, 400-room, noncasino hotel contained by the greater Mandalay Bay megaresort. The lobby area has a plush feel—a 1930s New York atmosphere that's very different (and pleasingly so) from Las Vegas in the new millennium. Off the lobby is a 60-seat sitting area and a second lounge that fronts the First Floor Grill gourmet room. And the Verandah Café is the most exclusive coffee shop in town. The pool has lush foliage, a spa, and cabanas.

The hotel's 400 rooms are on the 35th through 39th floors of the Mandalay Bay tower. Private express elevators deliver guests to their floors. Rates start at $250 for a superior king, but if you haggle, you can get a moderate king for less. Housekeepers provide turn-down service before bedtime.

The Four Seasons will appeal to ultra-upscale travelers looking for a minioasis that insulates them from the hullabaloo of Las Vegas. But it doesn't come cheaply. You're paying for the brandness as much as the grandness, and there are plenty of better values nearby (even in the same building).

Fremont

Sam Boyd's Fremont is a downtown landmark. It offers good food, budget lodging, and a robust, crowded casino. Table games are played beneath a high ceiling ringed in neon; slots cram narrow aisles. Locals, Asians, Hawaiians, and Southern Californians love the Fremont.

Frontier (The New)

The Frontier has been through the wringer . . . oops, make that the *New* Frontier. This is the hotel that essentially launched Siegfried & Roy in Las Vegas, the hotel with a super location smack in the middle of the Strip, and the hotel with owners who allowed it to get embroiled in a labor dispute and strike that lasted six and a half years. In 1998, Phil Ruffin bought the Frontier, quickly settled the strike, and christened the property the New Frontier. Since then, Ruffin has poured millions of dollars into repairs and improvements. The renovated guest rooms, new Chinese and Italian restaurants, and Gilley's Saloon stand out proudly. The New Frontier is staging a remarkable comeback. It is easily accessed from Fashion Show Drive or the Strip and is within easy walking distance of some of the best shopping in town.

Gold Coast

The Gold Coast, a half-mile west of the Strip, is a locals' hangout. There's no fantasy theme, but Gold Coast has the locals' favorite slots. The breakfast special is among the city's best, lounge entertainment is offered at all hours, and headliners and modest production shows are offered in the showroom. A movie complex and a huge bowling alley are available. Free transportation is provided to the hotel's sister property the Barbary Coast.

Gold Spike

About a four-minute walk from Fremont Street, the Gold Spike is basically a slot joint. It's congested and loud, luring customers with nickel and even penny slots.

Golden Gate

Devoted primarily to slots, the downtown Golden Gate is crowded and dingy but redeems itself by offering one of the city's best shrimp cocktail specials. The hotel has 106 budget rooms.

Golden Nugget

The flagship downtown hotel and one of the most meticulously maintained and managed properties in Las Vegas, the Golden Nugget is smack in the middle of Glitter Gulch. It offers bright, cheery rooms with tropical decor, first-rate showroom and lounge entertainment, excellent restaurants, a large pool, a spa, a shopping arcade, and a workout room. The casino is clean and breezy with white enameled walls. The feeling is upscale, though comfortable and informal.

Patrons come from New York, Dallas, Chicago, Los Angeles, and San Diego, as well as from Taiwan, Hong Kong, and Japan. Younger travelers (ages 28–39) like the Golden Nugget, as do older tourists and retirees.

Hard Rock Hotel

The Hard Rock is billed as the world's first rock-and-roll hotel and casino. Like the adjoining Hard Rock Cafe, it's loaded with rock memorabilia. Everywhere it's rock, rock, rock, from lounge music to piano-shaped roulette tables. Surprisingly tasteful guest rooms offer nice views. The Joint is Las Vegas's most intimate live-rock venue. Hard Rock targets baby boomers, younger Southern Californians, midwesterners, and urban northeasterners.

Harrah's Las Vegas

Unpretentious and upbeat Harrah's occupies the middle of the Strip's most prestigious block. Beyond tasteful guest rooms are a beautiful showroom, comedy club, and above-average restaurants and buffet. The L-shaped casino is bright and roomy, and the mood is lighthearted. Best of all, the staff, from dealers to desk clerks, is exceptionally friendly and helpful. Clientele tends to be older midwesterners, Southern Californians, and business and convention travelers.

Horseshoe

Binion's Horseshoe is an anchor in Glitter Gulch. The casino is large and active, with row upon row of slots clanking under a suffocatingly low ceiling. Table games are less congested. Old West–themed, the Horseshoe is one of the city's top spots for poker and craps. There's no maximum on wagers; bet a million if you wish. Locals and "real gamblers" hang out here.

Imperial Palace

The Imperial Palace has a large, active casino lavishly decorated with mammoth chandeliers and carved beams. *Legends in Concert,* one of Las Vegas's hottest shows, plays nightly, and the Imperial's auto museum is first-rate. No Las Vegas hotel has a better location; most guest rooms are Holiday Inn–quality. Embers restaurant can compete with top steakhouses.

The Imperial Palace offers the Strip's first medical clinic, with physicians available 24 hours every day. Any Las Vegas visitor can call (702) 893-6767.

Lady Luck

The Lady Luck downtown offers nice rooms or small suites at great prices. The large casino has wall-sized windows. If you're claustrophobic, this might be your place. The staff is personable and the atmosphere informal. Clientele includes Filipinos, Asian Americans, Californians, motor-coach tourists, and locals.

Las Vegas Club

A corridor linking the casino and sports bar at the sports-themed Las Vegas Club downtown is a veritable sports museum. The modest casino has some of the more player-friendly blackjack rules around. Request a room in the new North Tower. The property draws Hawaiians, midwesterners, bus groups, and seniors.

Las Vegas Hilton

Next to the Las Vegas Convention Center, the Hilton does more meeting, trade show, and convention business than any other hotel and provides a comfortable environment for its business clientele.

The Hilton operates under the valid assumption that many of its guests leave only to go to the Convention Center. Thus, the Hilton is an oasis of self-sufficiency, with recreation areas, a shopping arcade, a buffet, and excellent restaurants. The showroom hosts big name headliners. *Star Trek: The Experience,* an interactive video and virtual reality amusement center, features a spaceflight simulation.

The casino is huge but not formal or intimidating. The sports book is large and elegant. If you can afford it, the Hilton is the most convenient place to stay if you're a conventioneer. If you're here on pleasure, however, staying at the Hilton is luxurious exile. Anywhere you go, you'll need a cab or car, and self-parking can be 15 minutes from guest rooms.

Luxor

The Luxor is a 30-story pyramid with guest rooms around the interior sides from base to apex. Guest room hallways circumscribe a core containing the world's largest atrium, where elevators rise at a 39° angle from the pyramid's corners. While the interior is stunning, guests report it's easy to become disoriented. We seriously recommend carrying a small compass for finding your room.

Entry from the Strip is through a massive sphinx. Guests then are diverted into small entryways that open into the atrium. Rising imposingly within is an ancient Egyptian city. Around the inside base flows a "River Nile."

Straight ahead from the main entrance is the 100,000-square-foot casino. Open and attractive, it's tasteful by any standard. One level below is the main showroom. One floor above and reaching high into the atrium are structures representing the past, present, and future. In the future structure is a paid-admission attraction designed by Douglas Trumbull, creator of the *Back to the Future* ride at Universal Studios Florida, and an IMAX theater.

Flanking the pyramid are two new hotel towers. In all, Luxor offers 4,474 guest rooms, making it the city's second-largest hotel. Large, tasteful guest rooms are decorated in Egyptian motif with custom furniture. The only disappointment is that many don't have tubs.

Self-parking is a hassle. Valet parking is quick and efficient, worth the $1 or $2 tip. A moving walkway connects Luxor to Excalibur. Luxor is Circus Circus Enterprises' first serious effort to attract upscale, less family-oriented clientele.

Main Street Station

Main Street Station downtown accommodates overflow guests from the California across the street. The casino echoes a turn-of-the-century gentleman's club and contains enough antiques and art to furnish a museum. With refurbished guest rooms, a brew pub, and an excellent buffet, the property is interesting and fun.

Mandalay Bay

Circus Circus's Mandalay Bay opened in spring 1999 on the old Hacienda site. It's a megaresort in the true sense of the overworked word—3,700 guest rooms rank it as the fifth-largest hotel in Las Vegas. Mandalay Bay is a Burmese-themed clone of the Mirage, Treasure Island, and Bellagio. The sprawling complex features the 43-story, three-wing tower; an arena; a theater; a concert venue; a dozen restaurants; a water park; three large lounges; and the 400-room Four Seasons hotel. The signature spectacle is the four-story wine tower at Aureole.

Mandalay Bay appeals to a young, hip, fun-seeking, upscale market. All the different ideas jammed into Mandalay Bay might not always add up to a cohesive whole, but so many parts of the sum are unique that it makes for an interesting series of sights.

Maxim

The Maxim, a medium-sized hotel-casino, is nice, with renovated guest rooms. The casino is cramped but attractive. Restaurants and the buffet are good values. Maxim gets business from visitors attending meetings at the adjacent Bally's and is a favorite of seniors.

MGM Grand Hotel, Casino, and Theme Park

Elevation of MGM Grand's theme park to equal footing with its casino is the first significant tourism product diversification in Las Vegas since the dawn of luxury hotel-casinos in the '50s. Make no mistake, the theme park's purpose is to funnel patrons into the casino. What's different is that the theme park aims to attract nongamblers, too.

With the exception of Walt Disney World, the MGM Grand combines more facilities and recreational opportunities than any other U.S. resort. It offers both the nation's largest hotel (5,005 rooms) and the world's largest casino. The 112-acre complex includes a 33-acre movie- and entertainment-themed amusement park, a 15,200-seat special-events arena, 380,000 square feet of convention space, an enormous swimming area, four tennis courts, a spa, and a multilevel parking facility. An extensive electronic games arcade is supplemented by a "games of skill" midway. To this, MGM Grand is adding a 1,500-room Marriott Marquis, a 500-room Ritz-Carlton, an expanded casino, and a 6.6-acre pool and spa.

Entry from the Strip is beneath a 45-foot-tall MGM lion atop a 25-foot pedestal. The lion entrance leads to a domed rotunda with table games and the Rainforest Cafe, and from there to four huge casinos.

For practical purposes, the main entrance is a porte-cochere 15 lanes wide, serving vehicular traffic from Tropicana Avenue. Guests go directly into the hotel lobby with its 53 check-in windows and don't have to lug suitcases through the casinos. Congestion alert: Most pedestrians en route to the theme park also pass through this entrance and traverse the hotel public areas.

Beyond the elevators, a wide passageway leads to the theme park. Along it are five of MGM Grand's eight restaurants (not counting theme-park restaurants or fast food). The buffet (disappointing), 24-hour cafe, and pizza kitchen adjoin the casinos between the porte-cochere and lion entrances.

Live entertainment in the theme park is in addition to two showrooms. The 630-seat Hollywood Theater features headliners, and the 1,700-seat Grand Theater stages a high-energy production show. Comedy's on tap at Catch a Rising Star, and the casinos include four lounges. The arena accommodates boxing, tennis, rodeo, basketball, and major exhibitions.

A first at the MGM is a youth center providing supervised programs day and night for children (ages 3–12) of hotel guests. Unfortunately, only 50 or so children can be accommodated. Reserve two days in advance.

The MGM Grand Adventures Theme Park offers ten major

rides and attractions in eight themed areas, 10 restaurants and fast-food outlets, and a dozen retail shops (details on pages 146–48).

Guest rooms are comfortable but not luxurious. Standard rooms are decorated in movie themes, while rooms on higher floors have exceptional views. MGM Grand incorporated part of the MGM Marina Hotel, and rooms in the old structure aren't comparable in size or quality.

The MGM's biggest problem is weekend registration and checkout. Arriving guests inundate the check-in counter and queue up by the hundreds. To avoid this scene, arrive before noon Friday and arrange a late checkout Sunday.

The MGM Grand derives 80% of its business from individual travelers and tour groups. The affordable property is a natural for families. Geographically, it targets Southern California, Phoenix, Denver, Dallas, Houston, Chicago, and the Midwest.

Mirage

Exciting and compelling without being whimsical or silly, the Mirage blends the stateliness of marble with the exotic luxury of tropical greenery and polished bamboo. Casino, showroom, shopping, restaurants, and lounges are artfully integrated.

An atrium rainforest is the central hub. A 60-foot aquarium behind the front desk contains sharks, stingrays, and colorful tropical fish. In the entranceway from the Strip is a display of white Bengal tigers. Outside is a 55-foot-tall erupting volcano that disrupts traffic every quarter-hour in the evening. In addition are a live dolphin exhibit and a technologically advanced showroom. The production by illusionists Siegfried and Roy took Las Vegas entertainment (and prices) into the twenty-first century.

Restaurants are special, and bulk eaters will find an ample and affordable buffet. Amenities include a stunning swimming complex and stylish shopping arcade. The magnificent casino is huge yet informal. Guest rooms are among the city's nicest.

Although guests pay top dollar, the hotel isn't an exclusive retreat of the wealthy. It's also one of Clark County's top tourist attractions, creating a melting pot of wide-eyed humanity at all hours.

Monte Carlo

Its 3,002 guest rooms rank Monte Carlo as Las Vegas's seventh-largest hotel and the world's eighth-largest. It's modeled after the Place du Casino in Monte Carlo, Monaco, with ornate arches and fountains, and marble floors.

Guest rooms, with marble entryways and French period art, are mid- to upper-priced to compete with the MGM Grand. Amenities include a swimming complex with slides, wave pool, and float stream; an exceptional fitness center; an interesting shopping arcade; and a brew pub with live entertainment. The football-field-sized casino has simulated skylights and domes. The showroom is designed for illusionist Lance Burton.

Compared to the powerful settings of New York–New York, Treasure Island, and Luxor, the Monte Carlo's turn-of-the-century theme doesn't generate much excitement. But, Monte Carlo is an attractive hotel-casino rather than a crowded tourist attraction.

New York–New York

Although small by megaresort standards ("only" about 2,000 rooms), New York–New York triumphs in the realization of its theme. Guest rooms are in towers reminiscent of the Big Apple skyline, including the Empire State, Chrysler, and Seagrams buildings. The buildings are connected, but each offers different decor and ambience.

A half-sized Statue of Liberty and a replica of Grand Central Station lead visitors to one entrance, while the Brooklyn Bridge beckons to another. The property's interior is divided into themed areas, including Greenwich Village, Wall Street, and Times Square.

The casino looks like a movie set. Table games and slots are sandwiched between buildings, shops, restaurants, and well-executed city street facades.

Like its namesake, New York–New York is extremely congested and always awash with sightseers. Aisles and indoor paths are far too narrow to accommodate the crowds, and New York–New York succumbs periodically to pedestrian gridlock.

If you long for the thrill of a Big Apple cab ride, hop on the roller coaster. It's the fourth on the Strip but the only one where people on the street can hear riders scream. Our favorite New York–New York feature is Hamilton's, a cozy piano bar overlooking the casino.

Guest rooms approximate the Holiday Inn standard but are disappointing for a hotel with such a strong theme. Likewise, the swimming area and fitness center are only average. Full-service restaurants are above average and fast food quite interesting.

Nevada Palace

The Nevada Palace is a small Boulder Highway property patronized primarily by locals and seniors who use its RV park. Pleasant, with a new pool, two decent restaurants, and fair room rates, it's a less hectic alternative to downtown or the Strip.

Orleans

The 840-room Orleans, marketed primarily to locals, has a New Orleans/bayou theme executed in a cavernous building. The festive casino includes a two-story replication of a French Quarter street and a couple of nifty bars. Restaurants have little to do with the Louisiana theme. Upstairs is a 70-lane bowling complex. Recent additions include a movie complex and child-care center.

Palace Station

Palace Station is a local favorite that's beginning to attract tourists. With a top buffet, restaurants (crowded) offering amazing specials, a tower of handsome guest rooms, good prices, and access to downtown and the Strip, Palace Station has arrived. The railroad-themed casino is large and busy. Slots are reportedly loose. Lounge entertainment is first-rate.

Paris Las Vegas

Paris echoes its namesake, with a 50-story Eiffel Tower (with restaurant atop), an Arc de Triomphe, and a River Seine with boat rides. Thrown in for good measure are the Champs Elysée, Parc Monceau, and Paris Opera House.

Opened in September 1999, Paris offers 13 restaurants, shopping, a 25,000-square-foot spa, and an 85,000-square-foot casino.

Plaza

The Plaza is the only Las Vegas hotel with its own railroad station. Not long ago, the hotel was run-down, but tower rooms were renovated and are now available at very good prices. It's the only downtown hotel offering tennis and one of only two with showrooms. The restaurant looks straight down Glitter Gulch and the Fremont Experience; reserve a window table.

The table gaming area is very pleasant. Patrons include walk-ins, attendees of small meetings, and Southern Californians.

Quality Inn and Key Largo Casino

The Quality Inn is a great compromise. Although small, it has all the essentials (mini-casino, restaurant, gift shop). Every room has a wet bar and refrigerator. The crowning glory is an extraordinarily peaceful courtyard and pool complex.

Reserve

The Reserve, targeting locals, is a safari-themed hotel-casino southeast of Las Vegas. Although the theme is well executed, many people are reminded of a Rainforest Cafe with gambling. Available are a 42,000-square-foot casino, a popular lounge, a good buffet, several restaurants (try the steakhouse), and adequate guest rooms.

The Resort at Summerlin

The Resort at Summerlin is the first of several new upscale properties to offer a Scottsdale/Palm Beach resort experience as an alternative to the hype and madness of the Strip. Situated west of town near Red Rock Canyon, the Resort at Summerlin consists of two southwestern style hotels built around the TPC golf course. The resort offers a classy, comfortable casino with 1200 slots and 40 table games, an 11-acre gardens and interior courtyard area, and a large swimming complex. Restaurants serve oriental, continental, and beef fare respectively. There's also a buffet. Although the lounges, including an "Irish Pub" offer live entertainment, there is no showroom. While guest rooms are spacious and among the nicest in town, the real draw here is the golf and the spa. Guests include destination golfers, business travelers, and conference attendees.

Rio

The Rio is one of Las Vegas's treasures and our first choice for romantic getaways or honeymoons. Tastefully decorated in a Latin American carnival theme, it's a true destination resort. Rooms (all plush suites) offer exceptional views and cost the same as regular rooms at many other hotels.

The Rio has excellent restaurants, a great buffet, high-energy entertainment, a huge shopping arcade, and an elaborate swimming area. The casino includes a comfortable sports book.

Masquerade Village shopping venue, which surrounds the casino, offers "Masquerade in the Sky," a parade featuring floats and performers suspended from tracks high above the casino floor.

The Rio draws both locals and out-of-towners, particularly Southern Californians.

Riviera

Extending from the Strip halfway to the Las Vegas Convention Center, the Riviera accommodates both leisure and business travelers. It offers so much that many guests never leave the property. It has more long-running shows (four) than any other Las Vegas hotel and offers unusually varied entertainment, including production, striptease, female impersonator, and celebrity shows.

Some hotels serve better food, but few offer more variety, especially to the informal diner, who can choose among fast-food restaurants and the buffet. Amenities include a wedding chapel. Guest rooms, particularly in the towers, are surprisingly comfortable.

The huge casino is something of a maze. There's always noise, light, and activity. Walk-in traffic mixes with convention-goers, retirees on "gambling sprees," Asians, Asian Americans, and Southern Californians.

Sahara

The Moroccan-themed Sahara encompasses many buildings and towers. It offers a casino, convention hall, showroom, decent buffet, shopping arcade, two upscale restaurants, and swimming pool. It's remote, though, for anyone who wants to walk to the Strip, downtown, and the Convention Center.

Guest rooms are modern, and the new casino is visually exciting. Conventioneers, Southern Californians, and southwesterners predominate among patrons.

Sam's Town

Sam's Town is a rambling property with an Old West mining-town motif. In addition to the hotel and casino are a bowling alley, a very good buffet, one of Las Vegas's better Mexican eateries, a

steakhouse, a great '50s-style diner, an RV park, and a huge Western wear outlet. Locals throng the lounge featuring live country-
western music and dancing. A new events center and an 18-screen
movie theater will be added by early 2001.

A sports bar features pool, computerized golf, and half-court
basketball. At the atrium waterfall is a free but very well done
fountains-and-light show (watch the robotic wolf). Frequent customers include locals, seniors, and cowboys.

San Remo

The San Remo, across from the MGM Grand, traditionally attracts business travelers, Southern Californians, southwesterners,
and the Japanese.

It has a chandeliered casino, an OK restaurant, an average buffet, a great prime rib special, and a good sushi bar. Guest rooms
are well appointed.

Santa Fe

Bright and airy, with warm southwestern decor, the Santa Fe is
one of the city's more livable hotel-casinos. Guest rooms are nice
and a good value. Amenities include a spacious casino, above-
average buffet, lounge with live entertainment, bowling alley and,
amazingly, a hockey-sized ice-skating rink. The property targets
locals and tourists.

Showboat

A 100-lane bowling alley gives this property its informal, sporty
identity. The casino, busy but not overcrowded, includes an immense bingo parlor. Restaurants offer good value, and the buffet
is excellent. Lounge entertainment is good.

Silverton

Silverton has a nicely executed Old West mining theme. The
casino has rough-hewn beams, mine tunnels, overhead mine car
tracks, and mining artifacts. The buffet and coffee shop are above-
average. The lounge features country music and dancing. Silverton targets RVers with its large RV park.

Stardust

A five-minute walk from the Convention Center, the Stardust caters to conventioneers, tourists, and locals. Amenities include a shopping arcade. Restaurants are consistent and high-quality. Lounge entertainment is above-average, and the production show is excellent. The casino is vast.

Stratosphere

The 1,149-foot-tall Stratosphere Tower is the tallest building west of the Mississippi—taller than the Eiffel Tower (the real one). It houses indoor and outdoor observation decks, a revolving restaurant, four wedding chapels, and meeting rooms. The 360° view is breathtaking day and night. A hotel-casino is adjacent.

At the top of the tower are two thrill rides. The world's highest roller coaster is also the world's slowest and shortest. The other ride, however, called the Big Shot, is a monster: It rockets riders up the tower's needle with a force of four g's, then drops them back with no g's. And it all happens 1,000 feet in the air!

Texas Station

This North Las Vegas property catering to locals and cowboys is a sister to Palace, Sunset, and Boulder stations. The Western theme blends Texas ranch culture and Spanish architecture. Texas Station offers a 60,000-square-foot casino, seven restaurants, one of Las Vegas's best buffets, two bars, a dance hall, and a 12-screen movie theater.

Treasure Island

Lke the Mirage next door, Treasure Island is both hotel-casino and attraction, but it targets a younger, more middle-class family clientele.

Afternoons and evenings, a British man-of-war sails into the harbor and engages the pirate ship *Hispaniola* in a raging battle. Exceptional special effects and a cast of almost 80 pirates and sailors ensure that any Strip traffic not snarled by the Mirage's volcano will certainly be stopped by the shootout at sea.

Visitors entering the hotel from the Strip cross Buccaneer Bay on a plank bridge and transit a Caribbean pirate fort landscaped with palms. Through the main sally port is the commercial and residential area of Buccaneer Bay Village, complete with town square, shops, restaurants, and, of course, casino. To the usual slots and table games is added a comfortable sports book.

The hotel lobby and public areas are elaborate and detailed. The lobby bar, its patio lit by chandeliers made from cast-plastic human bones, is especially eye-catching. Pirate's Walk, the main interior passageway, leads to a shopping arcade, steakhouse, and buffet. The upscale Buccaneer Bay Club restaurant overlooks the sea battle.

Treasure Island is home to the extraordinary *Cirque du Soleil,* which performs in a custom-designed, 1,500-seat theater. Mutiny Bay is an electronic-games arcade for kids.

The beautiful swimming area has slides, waterfalls, grottos, and tranquil pools. Guest rooms are in a Y-shaped tower behind the pirate village. Decorated in earth tones, they provide a restful retreat from the bustling casino. Large windows afford a good view of the Strip or (on the west side) of the mountains and sunset.

Self-parking is easier than at most Strip hotels. An elevated tram connects Treasure Island and Mirage.

Tropicana

Of the four hotels at the intersection of the Strip and Tropicana (others are New York–New York, Excalibur, and MGM Grand), the Tropicana is the oldest. With its Paradise and Island Towers and 1,910 rooms, it offers a full range of services and amenities. It's also home to one of Las Vegas's most celebrated swimming complexes. The Sunday champagne brunch is among the city's best.

The bustling and bright casino ranks as one of the city's more pleasant and exciting places to gamble. Casino clientele is younger than average and includes guests from Excalibur enjoying the Trop's more-sophisticated style. It's particularly popular with slot players.

The guest rooms' tropical motif is exotic and in some cases includes mirrored ceilings. Views from the towers' upper rooms are among the city's best.

The Tropicana does a thriving business with wholesalers and bus tours and aggressively targets the Japanese and Hispanic markets. Southern Californians abound.

Vacation Village

The most remote property at the south end of the Strip, Vacation Village provides budget lodging and basic amenities. Guests find a nice southwestern-decor casino, pool, buffet, and Mexican restaurant. The property is friendly and welcomes families, but its isolation is a drawback.

The Venetian

The gargantuan Venetian development, across from Treasure Island, is being built in two phases. The first opened in spring 1999. The second will be the Lido Hotel and Casino. Bringing icons of world travel to Las Vegas (as have New York–New York, Mandalay Bay, and Paris Las Vegas), the Venetian replicates the plazas, architecture, and canals of Venice, Italy. The Campanile Tower, reached via the Rialto Bridge, is the resort's focal structure.

A re-creation of the Grand Canal passes beneath arched bridges and leads to a canopied version of St. Mark's Square. Along the canal are the 750,000-square-foot Grand Canal Shoppes, arranged beneath a vaulted-ceiling simulated sky.

Sixteen restaurants, most designed by noted chefs, provide a range of choices. Entertainment developed in partnership with *Billboard* magazine includes Billboard Live!, a combination dining and performance venue. Nightclubs in the complex will spotlight jazz, rock, country, and pop.

Rooms at the all-suite Venetian average 700 square feet. The sunken living room is equipped with fax machine/copiers with a dedicated phone line.

Although the Venetian says its bread-and-butter customers are business travelers and shoppers, it has included a 116,000-square-foot casino, larger than most Strip competitors'. When the Lido Casino comes on line, the resort will offer more than 200,000 square feet of casino, second only to the MGM Grand.

Westward Ho

A sprawling motel next to the Stardust, the Westward Ho offers a slots-oriented casino, lounge entertainment, a couple of pools, undistinguished dining, and good deals on drinks and snacks.

Suite Hotels

Suites

The term *suite* means many things in Las Vegas. Most suites are larger-than-average rooms with a conversation area (couch, chair, and coffee table) and a refrigerator. In a two-room suite, conversation and sleeping areas normally are separate. Two-room suites are not necessarily larger than one-room suites but are more versatile. One- and two-room suites cost about the same as a standard room.

Only the Rio and Venetian are all-suite properties.

A number of suite hotels don't have casinos. Patronized primarily by business travelers and nongamblers, they offer a quiet alternative to frenetic casino hotels. But because there's no gambling to subsidize operations, suites usually cost more at non-casino hotels.

Suite Hotels without Casinos

AmeriSuites

AmeriSuites offers large, but not luxurious, one-room suites at good prices. Amenities include a small fitness center, outdoor pool, and a few small meeting rooms. Continental breakfast is free.

Alexis Park

This is best known of Las Vegas's one- and two-room suite properties. Expensive and relatively exclusive, it offers most of the amenities of a large resort. Suites are upscale and plush, with southwestern decor. Staff is friendly and unpretentious. The Alexis park has filed a request to add a small casino; if this is a turn-off, call before you go. Guests include executive business travelers and Southern California yuppies.

Crowne Plaza Holiday Inn

Crowne Plaza suites (mostly two-room) are nicely appointed. There's a pool and cafe; ethnic restaurants are nearby.

Holiday Inn Emerald Springs

The pink stucco Holiday Inn offers moderately priced one- and two-room suites, plus a lounge, pool, and spa. Public areas and rooms are tranquil and sedate. The Veranda Cafe serves a breakfast buffet.

Mardi Gras Inn (Best Western)

The Mardi Gras offers Spartan suites at good rates. Quiet, with a well-manicured courtyard and pool, it's a short walk from the Convention Center. A coffee shop is on site. The "casino" is only a few slot machines.

Marriott Suites

Amenities are plentiful: outdoor pool and hot tub, fitness center, full-service restaurant, and room service. The small building is easy to navigate, and parking is convenient. Suites are tasteful.

Residence Inn

Across from the Convention Center, the Residence Inn by Marriott offers comfortable one- and two-bedroom suites with full kitchens and is more homelike than other suite properties. Amenities include a coin laundry.

St. Tropez

The St. Tropez offers beautifully decorated one- and two-room suites, often at less than $100 per night. Adjoining a small mall, St. Tropez provides a restaurant, lounge, pool, fitness center, VCRs in suites, and complimentary buffet breakfast. Most guests are upscale business travelers.

Las Vegas Motels

Because they compete with the huge hotel-casinos, many Las Vegas motels offer great rates or provide special amenities, including complimentary breakfast. National motel chains are well represented. We included some motels in the ratings and rankings section to indicate how these properties compare with hotel-casinos and all-suite hotels.

Hotel-Casinos and Motels: Rated and Ranked

Room Ratings

To separate properties according to the relative quality, tastefulness, state of repair, cleanliness, and size of standard room, we have grouped the hotels and motels in classifications denoted by

What the Ratings Mean		
★★★★★	*Superior Rooms*	Tasteful and luxurious by any standard
★★★★	*Extremely Nice Rooms*	What you would expect at a Hyatt Regency or Marriott
★★★	*Nice Rooms*	Holiday Inn or comparable quality
★★	*Adequate Rooms*	Clean, comfortable, and functional without frills—like a Motel 6
★	*Super Budget*	

stars. Our star ratings apply to Las Vegas properties only and don't necessarily correspond to ratings awarded by Mobil, AAA, or other travel critics.

Star ratings apply to room quality only and describe the property's standard accommodations: for most, a hotel room with either one king bed or two queen beds. In an all-suite property, the standard accommodation is either a one- or two-room suite. Amenities and location aren't factors in our ratings.

In addition to stars (which delineate broad categories), we also use a numerical rating system. Our rating scale is 0–100, with 100 as the best possible rating. Numerical ratings are presented to show the difference we perceive between one property and another.

How the Hotels Compare

In most hotels, the better rooms are in high-rise "towers." More modest "garden rooms" are found in one- and two-story outbuildings.

Because we can't check every room in a hotel, we inspect several randomly chosen rooms and base our rating on them. Inspections are conducted anonymously and without management's knowledge. It's possible that the rooms we inspect are representative but that by bad luck a guest is assigned an inferior room.

To avoid disappointment, investigate in advance. When you

make inquiries, obtain a photo of a hotel's standard room or a promotional brochure before you book. (Note: Some chains use the same guest room photo in their promotional literature for all hotels in the chain.) Ask how old the property is and when your room was last renovated. If you arrive and are assigned an inferior room, demand to be moved.

Cost estimates are based on the hotel's published rack rates for standard rooms, averaged between weekday and weekend prices. Each "$" represents $40. Thus a cost symbol of "$$$" means a room (or suite) at that property will cost about $120 a night.

These new hotels were not open when the Unofficial Guide went to press and aren't rated or ranked:

Paris Las Vegas, Ritz-Carlton at the MGM Grand, Aladdin, and the Resort at Lake Las Vegas.

Here's a comparison of the hotel rooms in town:

How the Hotels Compare

Hotel	Star Rating	Quality Rating	Cost ($=$40)
Caesars Palace (Palace Tower)	★★★★★	96	$$$$$$+
The Venetian	★★★★★	96	$$$$$$$–
Bellaggio	★★★★★	96	$$$$$$$+
Resort at Summerlin	★★★★★	95	$$$$$$$$$–
Desert Inn	★★★★★	94	$$$$+
Mandalay Bay	★★★★½	93	$$+
Four Seasons at Mandalay Bay	★★★★½	93	$$$$$$$+
Alexis Park	★★★★½	92	$$$$–
St. Tropez	★★★★½	92	$$$$
Mirage	★★★★½	91	$$$$
Rio	★★★★	88	$$$$$–
Las Vegas Hilton	★★★★	87	$$+
MGM Grand	★★★★	87	$$$
Hard Rock Hotel	★★★★	87	$$$$$–
Golden Nugget	★★★★	86	$$+
Bally's	★★★★	86	$$$$
Crowne Plaza	★★★★	85	$+
Marriott Suites	★★★★	84	$$$
Residence Inn by Marriott	★★★★	83	$$+
Harrah's (Carnival tower)	★★★★	83	$$$$$–
Stratosphere	★★★½	82	$$$–

How the Hotels Compare

Hotel	Star Rating	Quality Rating	Cost ($=$40)
Sunset Station	★★★½	82	$$$
New Frontier (Atrium Tower)	★★★½	82	$$$+
Flamingo Hilton	★★★½	81	$$$+
Orleans	★★★½	81	$$$+
Luxor	★★★½	81	$$$$–
Sam's Town	★★★½	80	$$
Treasure Island	★★★½	80	$$$$–
Monte Carlo	★★★½	80	$$$$
AmeriSuites	★★★½	80	$$$$+
Courtyard by Marriott	★★★½	79	$$+
Showboat	★★★½	77	$+
Harrah's (Mardi Gras tower)	★★★½	77	$$$$
California	★★★½	76	$$–
Stardust	★★★½	76	$$+
Palace Station	★★★½	75	$$$+
Santa Fe	★★★½	74	$$
Holiday Inn Emerald Springs	★★★½	73	$$
Main Street Station	★★★	73	$$+
Riviera	★★★	73	$$$
Comfort Inn South	★★★	72	$+
Bourbon Street	★★★	71	$+
Sunrise Suites	★★★	71	$$–
Holiday Inn Boardwalk	★★★	71	$$+
Barbary Coast	★★★	71	$$$+
Las Vegas Club (North Tower)	★★★	70	$
Horseshoe (East Wing)	★★★	70	$+
Sahara	★★★	70	$$
Circus Circus (tower rooms)	★★★	70	$$$–
Texas Station	★★★	70	$$$–
Lady Luck	★★★	69	$$
New York–New York	★★★	69	$$$$–
Imperial Palace	★★★	67	$+
Silverton	★★★	67	$+
Plaza	★★★	67	$+
Best Western Mardi Gras Inn	★★★	67	$$
Boulder Station	★★★	67	$$$
Tropicana	★★★	67	$$$
San Remo	★★★	67	$$$$–

How the Hotels Compare

Hotel	Star Rating	Quality Rating	Cost ($=$40)
Arizona Charlie's (Klondike Tower)	★★★	66	$+
Fairfield Inn	★★★	66	$$−
Fitzgeralds	★★★	66	$$
La Quinta (Paradise)	★★★	66	$$
Las Vegas Club (South Tower)	★★★	65	$
Sun Harbor Budget Suites	★★★	65	$$−
Sam Boyd's Fremont	★★★	65	$$−
Excalibur	★★★	65	$$$
Reserve	★★½	64	$$−
Quality Inn Key Largo	★★½	64	$$−
Best Western Heritage Inn	★★½	64	$$+
Days Inn Downtown	★★½	63	$$
Circus Circus (manor rooms)	★★½	63	$$+
Fiesta	★★½	62	$$−
Arizona Charlie's (Meadows Tower)	★★½	61	$+
Four Queens	★★½	61	$$−
El Cortez	★★½	60	$−
Nevada Palace	★★½	60	$+
Maxim	★★½	60	$$+
Best Western McCarran Inn	★★½	59	$$−
Howard Johnson Airport	★★½	59	$$
Gold Coast	★★½	59	$$$−
Royal Hotel	★★½	58	$
Sun Harbor Budget Suites	★★½	58	$$−
Days Inn Town Hall Casino	★★½	57	$$−
Casino Royale	★★½	56	$$+
Vacation Village	★★	53	$+
Westward Ho	★★	51	$+
Golden Gate	★★	50	$+
Travelodge Las Vegas Inn	★★	50	$+
Wild Wild West	★★	50	$+
Howard Johnson	★★	49	$+
Horseshoe (West Wing)	★★	48	$
Motel 6	★★	47	$$−
Gold Spike	★	31	$−

THE TOP 30 DEALS IN LAS VEGAS

Having listed the nicest rooms, let's reorder the list to rank the best combinations of quality and value in a room. Each property is awarded a value rating on a 0–100 scale. The higher the number, the better the value.

These ratings indicate value received for dollars spent. A ★★½ room at $30 may have the same value rating as a ★★★★ room at $85, but that doesn't mean the rooms will be comparable in quality. Regardless of whether it's a good deal, a ★★½ room is still a ★★½ room.

Here are the best room buys, regardless of location or star classification, based on averaged rack rates (a suite may cost less than a hotel room):

The Top 30 Best Deals in Las Vegas				
Hotel	Star Rating	Value Rating	Quality Rating	Cost ($=$40)
1. Crowne Plaza	★★★★	98	85	$+
2. Showboat	★★★½	96	77	$+
3. El Cortez	★★½	96	60	$−
4. Mandalay Bay	★★★★½	95	93	$$+
5. Comfort Inn South	★★★	95	72	$+
6. Las Vegas Club (North Tower)	★★★	95	70	$
7. Golden Nugget	★★★★	93	86	$$+
8. California	★★★½	92	76	$$−
9. Sam's Town	★★★½	89	80	$$
10. Las Vegas Club (South Tower)	★★★	89	65	$
11. Bourbon Street	★★★	89	71	$+
12. Las Vegas Hilton	★★★★	88	87	$$+
13. Horseshoe (East Wing)	★★★	88	70	$+
14. Santa Fe	★★★½	86	74	$$
15. Imperial Palace	★★★	85	67	$+
16. Silverton	★★★	85	67	$+
17. Arizona Charlie's (Klondike Tower)	★★★	84	66	$+
18. Residence Inn by Marriott	★★★★	84	83	$$+
19. Plaza	★★★	84	67	$+

The Top 30 Best Deals in Las Vegas (continued)

Hotel	Star Rating	Value Rating	Quality Rating	Cost ($=$40)
20. Sunrise Suites	★★★	82	71	$$–
21. Royal Hotel	★★½	81	58	$
22. Courtyard by Marriott	★★★½	78	79	$$+
23. Holiday Inn Emerald Springs	★★★½	75	73	$$
24. Marriott Suites	★★★★	71	84	$$$
25. Sun Harbor Budget Suites	★★★	70	65	$$–
26. Sam Boyd's Fremont	★★★	70	65	$$–
27. Alexis Park	★★★★½	69	92	$$$$–
28. Desert Inn	★★★★★	69	94	$$$$+
29. MGM Grand	★★★★	69	87	$$$
30. Lady Luck	★★★	69	69	$$

Leisure, Recreation, and Services Rating of Hotel-Casinos

Many Las Vegas visitors use their hotel rooms only as a depository for luggage and a place to nap or shower. These folks are far more interested in what the hotel offers in gambling, restaurants, live entertainment, services, and recreation.

Ranked below for breadth and quality of their offerings are hotels with full casinos. Using a weighted model, we calculated a composite Leisure, Recreation, and Services Rating. It doesn't factor in room quality. The rating should help you determine which properties provide the best overall vacation or leisure experience.

Interpreting the LR&S Ratings

Some hotels score low because they offer little entertainment, recreation, or food service. If the property is somewhat isolated, these deficiencies pose serious problems. If, on the other hand, a hotel is in a prime location, the shortcomings hardly matter.

Because the LR&S is a composite rating, its primary value is in identifying properties that offer the highest quality and greatest variety of restaurants, diversions, and activities. The rating doesn't indicate what those restaurants, diversions, or activities are.

LR&S Rating for Hotels with Full Casinos

Rank	Hotel	Leisure, Recreation & Services Rating
1	Bellaggio	97
2	Caesars Palace	96
3	Four Seasons at Mandalay Bay	94
4	Mandalay Bay	94
5	Mirage	93
6	The Venetian	90
7	Treasure Island	90
8	MGM Grand	89
9	Las Vegas Hilton	86
10	Desert Inn	85
11	Rio	85
12	Bally's	84
13	Flamingo Hilton	83
14	Luxor	83
15	Monte Carlo	81
16	New York–New York	80
17	Resort at Summerlin	80
18	Harrah's	79
19	Stratosphere	78
20	Tropicana	78
21	Hard Rock Hotel	77
22	Golden Nugget	75
23	Excalibur	74
24	Sunset Station	74
25	Circus Circus	73
26	Imperial Palace	72
27	Riviera	72
28	Stardust	71
29	Orleans	70
30	Sam's Town	70
31	Sahara	69
32	Texas Station	69
33	Main Street Station	68
34	Palace Station	67
35	Santa Fe	67
36	New Frontier	66

LR&S Rating for Hotels with Full Casinos (continued)

Rank	Hotel	Leisure, Recreation & Services Rating
37	Boulder Station	65
38	Fiesta	65
39	Gold Coast	64
40	Showboat	63
41	Lady Luck	62
42	Four Queens	61
43	Reserve	61
44	San Remo	60
45	Silverton	60
46	Barbary Coast	59
47	California	59
48	Westward Ho	59
49	Plaza	58
50	Maxim	57
51	Arizona Charlie's	56
52	Horseshoe	56
53	Sam Boyd's Fremont	55
54	Las Vegas Club	54
55	Holiday Inn Boardwalk	53
56	Fitzgeralds	51
57	Nevada Palace	51
58	Casino Royale	46
59	Wild Wild West	46
60	Bourbon Street	45
61	Days Inn Town Hall Casino	38
62	Vacation Village	38
63	El Cortez	31
64	Golden Gate	19
65	Gold Spike	13

When Only the Best Will Do

The trouble with profiles, including ours, is that details and distinctions are sacrificed in the interest of brevity and information accessibility. To distinguish the exceptional from the average, here are some best-of lists.

Best Dining (Expense No Issue)

Bellagio
Caesars Palace
Mandalay Bay
Venetian
Mirage
Rio
MGM Grand

Best Dining (for Great Value)

Texas Station
Fiesta
Main Street Station
California
Excalibur
Palace Station
Boulder Station
New Frontier
Rio
Sunset Station

Best Buffets

Bellagio
Resort at Summerlin
Main Street Station
Reserve Grand Safari
Fiesta
Orleans French Market
Bally's
Texas Station
Rio
Sunset Station

Best Champagne Brunches

Bally's
Bellagio
Circus Circus
Caesars Palace
MGM Grand
Fiesta
Sante Fe

Most Romantic Hotel-Casinos

Rio
Caesars Palace
Mirage
Mandalay Bay
Venetian
Resort at Summerlin

Best Guest Room Baths

Caesars Palace
Bellagio
Desert Inn
Venetian
Rio

Most Visually Interesting Casinos

Luxor
Venetian
Caesars Palace
Bellagio
Mandalay Bay
Mirage
New York–New York
Sunset Station
Rio
Hard Rock Hotel
MGM Grand

Best Views from Guest Rooms

Rio
Caesars Palace (Palace Tower)
Venetian (north view rooms)
Bellagio
Mandalay Bay/ Four Seasons
Stratosphere (upper south view rooms)

Tropicana (towers)
Hard Rock Hotel
New York–New York
Fitzgeralds

Best for Shopping On-Site or within a Four-Minute Walk

Caesars Palace
Venetian
Mirage
Treasure Island
Casino Royale
New Frontier
Harrah's

Best for Golf

Desert Inn
Resort at Summerlin

Best for Tennis

Desert Inn
MGM Grand
Bally's
Caesars Palace
Resort at Summerlin
Las Vegas Hilton
Flamingo
Plaza

Best for Bowling

Showboat
Gold Coast
Sam's Town
Orleans
Santa Fe

Best for Jogging or Running

Desert Inn
Mandalay Bay
Las Vegas Hilton

Best for Ice Skating

Santa Fe

Best Spas

Resort at Summerlin
Venetian
Caesars Palace
Bellagio
Mandalay Bay
Desert Inn
Mirage
Monte Carlo
Treasure Island
Luxor
Golden Nugget
MGM Grand

Best Swimming & Sunbathing

Mandalay Bay
Bellagio
Caesars Palace
Mirage
Venetian
Treasure Island
Tropicana
Flamingo
Monte Carlo
Hard Rock Hotel
Rio
Las Vegas Hilton
MGM Grand
Luxor
Resort at Summerlin
Desert Inn

Best for Weight Lifting, Nautilus, Stationary Cycling, Stair Machines, & Other Indoor Exercise Equipment

Venetian
Caesars Palace

Best for Indoor Exercise Equipment *cont'd*

Mandalay Bay
Bellagio
Mirage
Treasure Island
MGM Grand
Luxor

Desert Inn
Resort at Summerlin
Monte Carlo
Las Vegas Hilton
Bally's
Harrah's
Flamingo
Hard Rock Hotel

Putting the Ratings Together

To complete the picture for hotels with casinos, we combine the Room Quality Rating; the Room Value Rating; and the Leisure, Recreation, and Services Rating to derive an Overall Rating. Guest room considerations (quality and value) account for half of the Overall Rating, while the LR&S Rating accounts for the remaining half.

Overall Ratings				
Hotel	50% LR&S Rating	25% Quality Rating	25% Value Rating	100% **Overall Rating**
Mandalay Bay	94	93	95	94
Las Vegas Hilton	86	87	88	87
Mirage	93	91	64	85
Caesars Palace (Palace Tower)	96	96	46	84
MGM Grand	89	87	69	84
Bellaggio	97	96	40	83
Desert Inn	85	94	69	83
Golden Nugget	75	86	93	82
The Venetian	90	96	45	80
Four Seasons at Mandalay Bay	94	93	35	79
Treasure Island	90	80	47	77
Bally's	84	86	55	77
Sam's Town	70	80	89	77
Rio	85	88	46	76
Stratosphere	78	82	66	76
Showboat	63	77	96	75
Flamingo Hilton	83	81	51	74

Overall Ratings (continued)

Hotel	50% LR&S Rating	25% Quality Rating	25% Value Rating	100% **Overall** **Rating**
Luxor	83	81	48	74
Imperial Palace	72	67	85	74
Santa Fe	67	74	86	74
Sunset Station	74	82	60	73
Monte Carlo	81	80	44	72
Resort at Summerlin	80	95	34	72
Hard Rock Hotel	77	87	47	72
California	59	76	92	72
Harrah's (Carnival tower)	79	83	45	71
Stardust	71	76	66	71
Harrah's (Mardi Gras tower)	79	77	41	69
Orleans	70	81	51	68
Silverton	60	67	85	68
Las Vegas Club (North Tower)	54	70	95	68
Sahara	69	70	62	67
Main Street Station	68	73	61	67
Plaza	58	67	84	67
Horseshoe (East Wing)	56	70	88	67
New York–New York	80	69	34	66
Tropicana	78	67	40	66
Circus Circus (tower rooms)	73	70	48	66
Riviera	72	73	46	66
New Frontier (Atrium Tower)	66	82	52	66
Lady Luck	62	69	69	66
Las Vegas Club (South Tower)	54	65	89	66
Palace Station	67	75	51	65
Arizona Charlie's (Klondike Tower)	56	66	84	65
Texas Station	69	70	48	64
Excalibur	74	65	41	63
Circus Circus (manor rooms)	73	63	44	63
Fiesta	65	62	56	62
Bourbon Street	45	71	89	62
Reserve	61	64	58	61

Overall Ratings (continued)

Hotel	50% LR&S Rating	25% Quality Rating	25% Value Rating	100% **Overall Rating**
Sam Boyd's Fremont	55	65	70	61
Boulder Station	65	67	42	60
Four Queens	61	61	55	60
Arizona Charlie's (Meadows Tower)	56	61	65	59
Barbary Coast	59	71	41	58
Holiday Inn Boardwalk	53	71	53	58
Nevada Palace	51	60	68	58
Fitzgeralds	51	66	58	57
Gold Coast	64	59	34	55
San Remo	60	67	34	55
Westward Ho	59	51	50	55
Horseshoe (West Wing)	56	48	60	55
Maxim	57	60	42	54
El Cortez	31	60	96	54
Casino Royale	46	56	39	47
Wild Wild West	46	50	42	46
Days Inn Town Hall Casino	38	57	52	46
Vacation Village	38	53	48	44
Golden Gate	19	50	47	34
Gold Spike	13	31	32	22

Part Two

Entertainment and Nightlife

Las Vegas Shows and Entertainment

Las Vegas calls itself the "Entertainment Capital of the World." In the number of live productions staged daily, this is true. Plus, the standard of professionalism and value for your entertainment dollar is very high.

That having been said, here's the bad news: The average price of a ticket to one of the major production shows topped $50 in 1999, a whopping 80% increase since 1992. To balance the picture, however, the standard of quality for shows has likewise soared. And there's now literally something for everyone, from traditional Las Vegas feathers and butts to real Broadway musicals. Believe it or not, the value is still there. Maybe not in the grand showrooms and incessantly hyped productions, but in smaller showrooms and lounges and main theaters of off-Strip hotels.

Most Las Vegas live entertainment can be categorized as:

Celebrity Headliners	Impersonator Shows
Long-Term Engagements	Comedy Clubs
Production Shows	Lounge Shows

Celebrity Headliners   These concerts or shows feature big-name entertainers in a limited engagement, usually one to four weeks, but sometimes a single night. Big-name performers' shows cost $25 to $90.

Long-Term Engagements   These are shows by the famous and once-famous who have come to Las Vegas to stay.

Production Shows   These are continuously running, Broadway-style theatrical and musical productions. They feature chorus lines, elaborate choreography, and great spectacle. Usually playing twice nightly, six or seven days a week, production shows often run for years.

Usually, the show opens with an elaborate number featuring dancers or ice skaters and, often, topless showgirls. Magic or musical numbers then alternate with variety acts, including comics, jugglers, and balancing artists. The show ends with a spectacular finale.

Impersonator Shows   These are usually long-running shows featuring the impersonation of celebrities living (Joan Rivers, Cher, Neil Diamond, Tina Turner, Madonna) and dead (Marilyn Monroe, Elvis, Liberace). Generally, men impersonate male stars and women impersonate female stars.

Comedy Clubs   Stand-up comedy has a long tradition in Las Vegas. With the success of comedy clubs nationwide and the comedy club format on television, stand-up comedy in Las Vegas was elevated from lounges and production shows to its own venues. Las Vegas comedy clubs are small- to medium-sized showrooms featuring two to five comedians per show. Shows usually change each week, and they draw equally among tourists and locals. Most comics are young, and the humor is often raw and scatalogical.

Lounge Entertainment   Many casinos offer exceptional entertainment day and night in their lounges. Musical groups predominate. Reservations aren't required; if you like what you hear, walk in. (Sometimes there's a two-drink minimum for sitting in on a show.) Consult local visitor guides to find your preferred music.

They Come and They Go

Las Vegas shows come and go all the time. Don't be surprised if some of the shows reviewed in this guide are gone before you arrive.

Learn Who Is Playing before Leaving Home

Showguide is the Las Vegas Convention and Visitors Authority's entertainment calendar for all showrooms and many lounges. It lists hotels, tells who is playing and when, and lists reservation numbers. For a free copy, contact:

Las Vegas Convention and Visitors Authority
Visitor Information Center
3150 Paradise Road
Las Vegas, NV 89109-9096
(702) 892-7576

Show Prices and Taxes

Admission to shows ranges from around $15 to $100 or more per person. At dinner shows, dinner is extra. Prices usually don't include taxes (17%) or server gratuities. A $20 ticket with tax and tip can cost $27 or more; a $50 ticket, $63 and beyond.

As recently as 1990, reserved seats were nonexistent. You made your reservation, then arrived early to be assigned a seat by the showroom maître d'. (Slipping the maître d' a tip ensured a better seat.) Typically, the show price included two drinks, and you paid at your table. The current trend is toward reserved seating. Seats are assigned when you buy your tickets at the casino box office or by phone with your credit card. At the showroom, an usher takes you to your seats.

If there are two performances per night, the early show is often more expensive. Some shows add a "surcharge" on Saturdays and holidays.

Showrooms sometimes offer deals. Look for ads or coupons in local tourist magazines or casino funbooks (see page 134). Ask about deals and discounts when you call for show or lodging reservations.

How to Make Reservations for Las Vegas Shows

Almost all showrooms take phone reservations. Either you call the reservation numbers we list, or your hotel concierge calls. Most shows accept reservations at least one day in advance.

Some shows take only your name and the number of people in your party. You pay at the box office on the day of the show or in the showroom after you're seated.

Increasingly, shows allow you to prepurchase tickets by phone using a credit card, and you then pick up your tickets at the box office before the show.

Hotel Lobby Ticket Sales

The phone reservation system works perfectly, but some folks prefer to buy tickets at booths operated by independent brokers in hotel lobbies. These visitors pay substantial booking and gratuity surcharges and discover at the showroom that the ticket doesn't guarantee reserved seating. Further, at several showrooms, these tickets must be exchanged for one of the showroom's tickets—after another wait in line.

Booths selling seats only for shows at that hotel-casino won't add surcharges.

Trying to See a Show without a Reservation or Ticket

Sunday through Thursday, you have a fair shot at getting into most shows by asking the maitre d' to seat you or by purchasing a ticket at the box office. On most Fridays and Saturdays, however, don't wait in line at the showroom entrance to inquire. Go directly to the box office, maître d', or other show personnel and ask if there's room for your party. You may be asked to join the end of the line or to wait while they check for no-shows or cancellations. An amazing percentage of the time, you'll be admitted.

DINNER SHOWS VS. COCKTAIL SHOWS

For some early shows (7–8 p.m. show times) you can choose between a cocktail show and a dinner show. Usually the show begins about 8 p.m. If you choose dinner, you must arrive for seating by 6 p.m., enabling you to be fed and the table cleared before show time. Cocktail show admission usually includes two drinks; seating is an hour before show time. Shows at 9 p.m. or later are exclusively cocktail shows. (Dinner patrons often get better seats.)

With all dinner shows, drinks will be extra—and invariably expensive. Food quality is generally acceptable.

Early vs. Late Shows

If you attend a late show, you have time for a leisurely dinner before the performance. If you prefer to eat late, the early show followed by dinner works better. Both shows are identical except that for some productions the early show is covered and the late is topless.

PRACTICAL MATTERS
What to Wear to the Show

Guests tend to dress up when they go to a show. For performances in the main showrooms at Bally's, Bellagio, Caesars Palace, the Las Vegas or Flamingo Hiltons, the Desert Inn, Mandalay Bay, the Tropicana, or the Mirage, men wear sport coats, with or without neckties. At the Las Vegas Hilton, Venetian, and Bally's, men often wear suits. Women generally wear suits, dresses, skirt and blouse/sweater combinations, or semiformal attire.

Showrooms at the Luxor, Stratosphere, Monte Carlo, New York–New York, Treasure Island, MGM Grand, Harrah's, Rio, Aladdin, Maxim, Riviera, Sahara, and Stardust are less dressy (sport coats, slacks, and sweaters or sport shirts are acceptable for men). Showrooms at the Excalibur, Imperial Palace, Orleans, House of Blues at Mandalay Bay, Golden Nugget, and Hard Rock are the least formal (come as you are). All comedy clubs are informal.

Invited Guests and Line Passes

At the showroom, guests line up to be seated. At showrooms with reserved seats, patrons are ushered to their seats. At those without, guests normally encounter two lines. The shorter is where "Invited Guests" (gamblers staying at that casino) queue up for immediate seating. Some have been given "comps" (complimentary admission) to the show. If you're giving the casino a lot of action, request a comp.

Gamblers or hotel guests of more modest means frequently receive line passes. These guests pay the standard price for the show but are admitted through the Invited Guest line. To obtain a line pass, tell the floorman or pit boss that you have been gambling a fair amount in their casino and have show reservations. Ask for a line pass. You'll probably get one, especially Sunday through Thursday.

Invited guests should arrive 30 minutes before show time.

Reservations, Tickets, and Maître d' Seating

Many showrooms practice maître d' seating. This means no seats are reserved, except for certain invited guests. When you call for tickets, you'll be listed on the reservations roster, but you won't

Showrooms Where Self-Parking Is Easy and Convenient

| Hard Rock | Orleans | San Remo |
| Desert Inn | Stratosphere | |

receive a seat until you appear before the maître d'. At some show-rooms, you pay your waiter for everything (show, taxes, drinks) after you have been seated and served.

At comedy clubs and an increasing number of showrooms, you go first to a booth labeled "Tickets," "Reservations," "Box Office," or "Guest Services." After the attendant verifies your reservation, you pay and receive a ticket to show the maître d'. This replaces paying at your table (unless drinks aren't included). The ticket usually doesn't reserve a specific seat or include gratuities.

Showrooms increasingly are switching from maître d' seating to "box office" or "hard" seating. Seat assignments are printed on tickets. Most showrooms issuing reserved-seat tickets allow you to charge them by phone using your credit card, but the quality of seating is at the mercy of the box office. If you buy tickets in person at the box office, however, you can pick among available seats.

Where to Sit

The best seats in most showrooms are the roomy booths that provide an unencumbered view of the show. The vast majority of seats, however, are at banquet tables—long, narrow tables where a dozen or more guests are squeezed together.

Banquet-table seating generally is right in front of the stage. Next, on a higher tier, is a row of plush booths. These are often reserved for the casino's best customers (sometimes for big tippers). Behind the booths but on the same level are more banquet tables. The pattern continues to the rear wall.

For big production shows on a wide stage (*Siegfried & Roy, Cirque du Soleil,* etc.) or for musical concerts, sit in the middle and back a little. For smaller shows on medium-sized stages (*Lance Burton, Legends in Concert,* etc.), up front is great. This is also true for headliners like Bill Cosby. For female impersonators, the illusion is better if you're back a bit.

At comedy clubs and smaller shows, there are no bad seats, though you'll want to avoid the columns at the Tropicana's *Comedy Stop*. Note: Comedians often incorporate guests sitting down front into the act.

Getting a Good Seat at Showrooms with Maître d' Seating

1. Arrive early   This is particularly important Friday and Saturday.

2. Go on an off-night (Sunday through Thursday)   During citywide conventions, weekdays may also be crowded.

3. Know where you would like to sit   State your preferences.

4. Understand your tipping options   You have three:

- Don't tip.

- Tip the maître d'.

- Tip the captain instead of the maître d'.

Don't tip   Politely request a good seat instead of tipping. This option works better in all but a few showrooms, particularly Sunday through Thursday.

On slower nights, the maître d' often distributes patrons equally throughout the showroom to make the audience look larger. On these nights, you may get preferred seats simply by asking.

Tip the maître d'   The maître d' is the man or woman in charge of the showroom. Maître d's in better showrooms are powerful and wealthy; some take in as much as $1,650 a night.

If you arrive early and tip $15–20 (per couple) in major showrooms or $5–10 in smaller rooms, you should get decent seats. Tip more on weekends or at popular or sold-out shows. If you arrive late on a busy night, ask if good seats remain before you tip.

Have your tip folded in your hand when you reach the maître d'. Arrange it so he can see how much it is. State your seating preference as you inconspicuously place the bills in his palm.

A variation is to tip with an appropriate denomination of the casino's chips. They cost the same as currency and imply you have been gambling with that denomination. This gesture makes you an insider and a more valued customer.

Tip the captain   Tell the maître d' where you would like to sit, but don't offer a tip. Follow the captain to your seats. If they're good, you haven't spent an extra nickel. If you'd like something better, tip the captain and ask to be moved or to have unoccupied seats you see that you prefer.

Before the Show Begins

For years, admission to cocktail shows included two drinks. Recently, this policy has been in flux. Variations are: a cash bar and no table service (to get a drink before the show, walk to the bar and buy it) or drinks included but no table service (exchange your receipt at the bar for drinks).

Most other showrooms offer table service. You obtain drinks from a server. If they're included, the captain will put a receipt or other documentation at your place when you're seated. The server takes it when you order drinks. If drinks aren't included, a menu lists prices.

If you're the last seated at a table, don't worry. Your server *will* notice.

Depend on your server to advise you when it's time to settle your tab. Until then, don't offer a tip. Most showrooms accept cash, major credit cards, and traveler's checks.

If you have prepaid for admission and drinks, your gratuity may be included. If not, tip the server a dollar or two per person when your drinks arrive. If you aren't sure what's included, ask.

Bladder Matters   Most showrooms don't have a rest room. The nearest one may be across the casino. Allow at least 10 minutes for the round trip.

Selecting a Show

Choosing a Las Vegas show is a matter of timing, budget, taste, and schedule (showrooms are dark/closed some days).

Older visitors are often more affluent than younger ones. So, most celebrity headliners are chosen, and most production shows created, to appeal to people age 40 and older.

Baby boomers are a primary market for Las Vegas. Stars from the "golden days" of rock and roll, plus folk singers from the 60s, play the city regularly.

Visitors younger than 35 years will still enjoy production

shows, though the cultural orientation and music will seem a generation or two removed. Several shows, however, have achieved a more youthful presentation: *Splash* (Riviera), *Cirque du Soleil's Mystere* (Treasure Island), *Cirque du Soleil's "O"* (Bellagio), *Spellbound* (Harrah's), *Lance Burton* (Monte Carlo), *Lord of the Dance* (New York–New York), *Chicago* (Mandalay Bay), and *Forever Plaid* (Flamingo). Also, comedy clubs are more youth-oriented.

LAS VEGAS SHOWS FOR THE UNDER-21 CROWD

Shows spotlighting magic, circus acts, impersonation, and period entertainment are appropriate for younger viewers. Many celebrity headliner shows are fine for children, and a few production shows offer a covered early show for families. Some topless production shows bar anyone younger than 21. Comedy venues usually admit teenagers accompanied by an adult.

The Best Shows in Town: Celebrity Headliners

The talent, presence, drive, and showmanship of many Las Vegas headliners often exceed all expectations, and even performers you think you wouldn't like will delight and amaze you. Also, don't hesitate to take a chance on a headliner unfamiliar to you.

Here are major celebrity showrooms and their regular headliners.

Caesars Palace Circus Maximus Showroom

Reservations and Information: 731-7333 or (800) 445-4544

Frequent Headliners: Julio Iglesias, Jay Leno, David Copperfield, Reba McEntire, Johnny Mathis, Jerry Seinfeld, Natalie Cole, Ray Charles, Wynonna Judd, Tony Bennett

Usual Show Times: Varies   *Dark:* Varies

Approximate Admission: $55–80, plus $2.50 surcharge per ticket

Drinks Included: None

Showroom Size: 1,050 persons

Comments   Large showroom with four levels; visibility generally excellent. Banquet table seating extremely crowded. Most headliners work one- or two-week engagements several times each year.

Consumer Tips Pay at the table for beverages. If you self-park, allow 10 minutes to reach the showroom. Rest rooms are far from the showroom.

Desert Inn Crystal Room

Reservations and Information: 733-4566

Frequent Headliners: Buddy Hackett, Gordon Lightfoot, Rita Rudner, Dennis Miller

Usual Show Times: 9 p.m.   *Dark:* Varies

Approximate Admission: $41–53, tax included

Drinks Included: None

Showroom Size: 751 persons

Comments Veteran performers alternate with oldies rock stars, contemporary country stars, and short- to medium-run production shows.

Consumer Tips Unusually low stage best suited to celebrity headliners and musical groups. Maître d' seating. Admission paid tableside. Children age 5 and older are admitted with adult.

Hard Rock Hotel—The Joint

Reservations and Information: 693-5066 or 226-4650

Frequent Headliners: Top current and oldies rock, pop, blues, folk, and world music stars

Usual Show Times: 8 p.m.

Approximate Admission: $15–125

Drinks Included: None

Showroom Size: 1,400 persons

Comments Performers include Bob Dylan, the Black Crowes, Melissa Etheridge, the Eagles, and Seal. Engagements are short; each is a special event. On the floor, 1,000 reserved-seat patrons are tightly packed around small tables; visibility is good. Acoustics are excellent, especially in the middle of the floor and the front of the balcony.

Consumer Tips Although we avoid them, about 400 "standing-room" tickets are sold when the reserved seats are gone (or if someone *wants* to stand). SRO patrons are put at the back of the floor, the back of the balcony (limited visibility), or in "the pit." Stage-side, be prepared for ear-splitting, bone-quaking acoustics and intense crowding.

Mandalay Bay—House of Blues

Reservations and Information: 632-7777 or (877) 632-7400

Frequent Headliners: Current and former pop, rock, R&B, reggae, folk, and country stars

Usual Show Times: 8 and 10 p.m.

Approximate Admission Price: $7–92

Drinks Included: None

Showroom Size: 1,800 seats

Description and Comments   This new Las Vegas concert hall is more like an opera house (than the high school-gym Joint): low ceiling, multitiered, and split-leveled, which gets the audience as close in to the act as possible. Live music is presented almost every night of the year. Recent performers have included BB King, the Go-Go's, Chris Isaak, Ziggy Marley, and De la Soul.

Consumer Tips   House of Blues ticket agents are extremely difficult to get by telephone; to save yourself an exorbitant phone bill, use the toll-free number listed above (and press 4). The box office is open 8 a.m. to 11 p.m.; the best time to call is right at 8 a.m.

MGM Grand—Garden Arena

Reservations and Information: 891-7777 or (800) 646-7787

Frequent Headliners: National acts, superstars, televised boxing, wrestling, and other sporting events

Usual Show Times: Varies   *Dark:* Varies

Approximate Admission: Varies

Drinks Included: None

Showroom Size: 15,200

Comments   Championship boxing matches and big-name musical concerts are favorites at the arena.

Consumer Tips   Buy reserved-seat tickets through reservations or Ticketmaster outlets (phone (702) 474-4000). If you aren't an MGM Grand guest, arrive by cab or allow extra time to reach the arena.

MGM Grand—Hollywood Theater

Reservations and Information: (800) 646-7787

Frequent Headliners: Righteous Brothers, Liza Minnelli, Sheena
  Easton, Tom Jones, Don Rickles, Rodney Dangerfield, Engle-
  bert Humperdink

Usual Show Times: Varies   *Dark:* Varies

Approximate Admission: $47–78

Drinks Included: None

Showroom Size: 630 persons

Comments   All seats front-facing. Engagements usually one to
three weeks.

Consumer Tips   Most presentations allow children. If you aren't
an MGM Grand guest, arrive by cab or allow extra time to reach
the showroom.

Mirage—Theatre Mirage

Reservations and Information: 792-7777

Frequent Headliners: Siegfried & Roy, Bill Cosby, Kenny Rogers,
  Paul Anka

Usual Show Times: Varies with performers; 7:30 and 11 p.m. for
  Siegfried & Roy

Dark: Wednesday and Thursday (for *Siegfried & Roy*)

Approximate Admission: $55–90

Drinks Included: 2 (taxes and gratuities also included)

Showroom Size: 1,500 persons

Comments   The *Siegfried & Roy* show is featured most of the year.
When they're off, other headliners take one- or two-week stands.
One of the city's most modern showrooms; every seat offers good
visibility.

Consumer Tips   Although it's assigned seating, no reservations are
taken for any show. Buy tickets one to three days in advance at the
Mirage box office. Hotel guests may charge tickets to their room.

Orleans—Orleans Showroom

Reservations and Information: 365-7075

Frequent Headliners: Crystal Gayle, Rich Little, The Smothers
  Brothers

Usual Show Times: Varies   *Dark:* Varies

Approximate Admission: Varies

Drinks Included: None

Showroom Size: 800 persons

Comments   Tiered theater seats in crescent around the stage. Designed for solo performers and bands. Good visibility everywhere. Lineup concentrates on country-western celebrities.

Consumer Tips   Great talent at bargain prices. All seats reserved.

Production Shows

LAS VEGAS PREMIER PRODUCTION SHOWS: COMPARING APPLES AND ORANGES

Las Vegas production shows are difficult to compare, and audience tastes differ. That said, our rankings reflect our favorites among continuously running shows. This apples-and-oranges comparison is based on each show's impact, vitality, originality, pace, continuity, crescendo, and ability to entertain.

Some shows are better than others, but there aren't any real dogs.

Production Show Hit Parade

We don't rate short-run engagements (comedy clubs, comedy theater, and celebrity headliners) and afternoon-only shows. Those we rate also receive a Value Rating:

A Exceptional value, a real bargain

D Somewhat overpriced

B Good value

F Significantly overpriced

C Absolutely fair, you get exactly what you pay for

(Prices in the '90s have soared more than 50%, and bargains are few.)

PRODUCTION SHOW PROFILES

Here are profiles of all continuously running production shows, alphabetically by show name. Comedy clubs and celebrity

	Production Show Hit Parade		

Rank	Show	Location	Value Rating
1.	*Cirque du Soleil's Mystere*	Treasure Island	B
2.	*Cirque du Soleil's "O"*	Bellagio	D
3.	*Chicago*	Mandalay Bay	C
4.	*EFX*	MGM Grand	C
5.	*Siegfried & Roy*	Mirage	F
6.	*Danny Gans*	Rio	F
7.	*Caesars Magical Empire*	Caesars Palace	B
8.	*Legends In Concert*	Imperial Palace	B
9.	*Lance Burton*	Monte Carlo	C
10.	*Forever Plaid*	Flamingo	A
11.	*Steve Wyrick*	Lady Luck	B
12.	*Enter the Night*	Stardust	B
13.	*Imagine*	Luxor	B
14.	*Jubilee*	Bally's	C
15.	*The Great Radio City Music Hall Spectacular*	Flamingo	B
16.	*Folies Bergere*	Tropicana	C
17.	*American Superstars*	Stratosphere	A
18.	*Splash*	Riviera	C
19.	*Spellbound*	Harrah's	C
20.	*Tournament of Kings*	Excalibur	B
21.	*La Cage/Kenny Kerr*	Riviera/Plaza	B
22.	*Crazy Girls*	Riviera	C

headliner showrooms are profiled in separate sections. Prices fluctuate.

American Superstars

Type of Show: Celebrity impersonator production show

Host Casino and Showroom: Stratosphere—Broadway Showroom

Reservations and Information: 382-4446 (reservations necessary)

Admission with Taxes: $25.50

Cast Size: About 24

Nights of Lowest Attendance: Sunday, Monday

Usual Show Times: 7 and 10 p.m.   *Dark:* Thursday

Topless: No

Author's Rating: ★★★½

Overall Appeal by Age:

Under 21	21–37	38–50	51 and older
★★★	★★★½	★★★★	★★★½

Duration: Hour and a half

Comments   Similar to *Legends in Concert* (Imperial Palace), but not as crisp or realistic. Impersonated stars include Madonna, Michael Jackson, Gloria Estefan, Spice Girls, and Elvis. Impersonators do their own singing. They're frequently upstaged by energetic dancers. Still, it's a great night's entertainment.

Consumer Tips   Tickets must be purchased in advance. Maître d' seating. Drinks at bar outside showroom.

Caesars Magical Empire

Type of Show: Magic and illusion dinner show

Host Casino and Showroom: Caesars Palace—Caesars Magical Empire

Reservations and Information: 731-7333 or (800) 445-4544 (reservations necessary)

Admission with Taxes: $75 adults

Cast Size: About 20

Nights of Lowest Attendance: Monday, Tuesday

Usual Show Times: Continuous daily from 4:30 p.m.

Special Comments: Best dinner-show food in town

Dark: Wednesday, Thursday

Topless: No

Author's Rating: ★★★★

Overall Appeal by Age:

Under 21	21–37	38–50	51 and older
★★★★	★★★★	★★★★	★★★★

Duration   About 3–3½ hours to eat and see everything

Comments   Best dinner entertainment package in Las Vegas. It's part restaurant, part attraction, and part stage show. Diners enter chambers where a magician entertains as they eat. Several main courses are offered. After dining, guests wait in a rotunda until they're called into one of two theaters. A smaller theater features sleight of hand. The other offers eye-popping illusions on the David Copperfield scale. After seeing both shows, guests exit into the casino.

Consumer Tips   Magic and illusion are as good as anywhere in Las Vegas. Considering it costs $15 less than *Siegfried & Roy and* includes an excellent dinner with wine, it's virtually unbeatable. Prepaid advance reservations are required. The Magical Empire is open from 4:30 p.m., but discounts of $10 per person are available to those who tour between 10:45 a.m. and 3:45 p.m. Mixed drinks are sold in the rotunda. Everything is on a schedule; there are no cocktails before dinner or much lingering afterward.

Chicago

Type of Show: Broadway musical

Host Casino and Showroom: Mandalay Bay—Mandalay Bay Theater

Reservations and Information: 632-7580

Admission with Taxes: $61, $72, $83

Cast Size: 24

Nights of Lowest Attendance: Monday, Tuesday

Usual Show Times: 7:30 p.m.

Topless: No

Author's Rating: ★★★★★

Overall Appeal by Age:

Under 21	21–37	38–50	51 and older
★★	★★★★	★★★★	★★★★

Duration: 2 hours and 20 minutes, with a 15-minute intermission

Comments   *Chicago* could be the best show in town, both because it's perfect for Las Vegas and at the same time so antithetical to the Las Vegas–style show. This Ebb and Kander musical is an updated revival of the original *Chicago* that opened on Broadway in 1975. Taking place in the jazz-vaudeville era of the 1920s,

Chicago is done mostly in black and white and involves a chorus girl who murders a lover and goes to jail; the bulk of the action takes place in the women's lock-up.

The theme of *Chicago* is ultra cynical and the mood is very dark, but the rest of the presentation is A-list all the way. Staging is minimal—there's no scenery at all, and props are limited.

Consumer Tips The floor and lower mezzanine seats are all good, but the upper mezzanine is pretty far away, especially for the price. If you go, spring for the extra $10 or $20 for the better seats. Order tickets in advance at the Mandalay Bay box office or at Ticketmaster (phone (702) 474-4000). There is no cancellation policy—if you buy 'em you own 'em. You're required to show your confirmation number and a photo ID when you pick up your tickets. Drinks are available at the bar in the theater. At intermission, it's best to pick up a re-entry pass and head into the casino, where there's a bigger rest room.

Cirque du Soleil's Mystere

Type of Show: Circus as theater

Host Casino and Showroom: Treasure Island—*Cirque du Soleil* Showroom

Reservations and Information: 894-7722 or (800) 392-1999

Admission with Taxes: $70 adults; $35 children (ages 11 and younger)

Cast Size: 75

Nights of Lowest Attendance: Thursday

Usual Show Times: 7:30 and 10:30 p.m.   *Dark:* Monday and Tuesday

Special Comments: No table service (no tables!)

Topless: No

Author's Rating: ★★★★1/2

Overall Appeal by Age:

Under 21	21–37	38–50	51 and older
★★★★	★★★★★	★★★★★	★★★★½

Duration: Hour and a half

Comments *Mystere* is the most difficult show in Las Vegas to describe. *Cirque du Soleil* is much more than a circus, though its players could perform with distinction in any circus. It combines elements of classical Greek theater, mime, the English morality play, surrealism, and comedy. The show pivots on its humor, sometimes black, and engages the audience with unforgettable characters. As you laugh and watch the amazingly talented cast, you are moved and soothed as well as excited and entertained. *Mystere* is a must-see.

Consumer Tips At almost any time, audience members might be plucked from their seats to participate. If you don't want to get involved, politely decline. Spectators can buy refreshments at concession stands.

Cirque du Soleil's "O"

Type of Show: Circus and aquatic ballet as theater
Host Casino and Showroom: Bellagio—Bellagio Theater
Reservations and Information: 693-7722
Admission with Taxes: $100 main floor; $90 balcony
Cast Size: 74
Nights of Lowest Attendance: Sunday and Monday
Usual Show Times: 7:30 and 11 p.m.   *Dark:* Wednesday and Thursday
Topless: No
Author's Rating: ★★★★
Overall Appeal by Age:

Under 21	21–37	38–50	51 and older
★★★★	★★★★★	★★★★★	★★★★½

Duration: Hour and a half

Comments The title *"O"* is a play on words derived from the concept of infinity, with 0 as its purest expression, and from the phonetic pronunciation of *eau,* the French word for water. Both symbols are appropriate. The production creates a timeless dream state and also incorporates an aquatic dimension that figuratively and literally evokes all meanings of water. The aquatic theater where *"O"* resides is no less than a technological triumph. *"O"* imparts a global impact that envelops you and holds you suspended. In the end you have a definite sense that you *felt* what transpired rather than having merely seen it. Though *"O"* is brilliant, it lacks a bit of the humor, accessibility, and poignancy of *Cirque's Mystere*. However, if you enjoyed *Mystere*, you will also like *"O,"* and vice versa. Though the productions share stylistic similarities, they are quite different.

Consumer Tips If you've never seen either of the Las Vegas *Cirque du Soleil* productions, we recommend catching *Mystere* first—it's $30 per person less expensive and just as good. *"O"* is a great show, and if you decide to shell out $100 ($90 for balcony seats) per ticket, you should buy tickets using your credit card over the phone before you leave home. If you decide to see *"O"* at the spur of the moment, try the box office about 30 minutes before show time. Sometimes seats reserved for comped gamblers will be released for sale.

Crazy Girls

Type of Show: Erotic dance and adult comedy

Host Casino and Showroom: Riviera—Mardi Gras Showrooms, second floor

Reservations and Information: 794-9301 or (800) 634-3420

Admission with Taxes: $24 (includes 2 drinks)

Cast Size: 8

Nights of Lowest Attendance: Wednesday, Thursday

Usual Show Times: 8:30 and 10:30 p.m., with a midnight show on Saturdays

Dark: Monday

Topless: Yes

Author's Rating: ★★★½

Overall Appeal by Age:

Under 21	21–37	38–50	51 and older
N/A	★★★½	★★★½	★★★½

Duration: Hour and 10 minutes

Comments A show for men who don't want to sit through jugglers or magicians before they see naked women. Eight engaging, talented, and athletically built young ladies bump and grind in exotic dance and comedy. Choreography is creative, the performance fast-paced.

Consumer Tips   The show is not as dirty as the Riviera would lead you to believe, and the nudity doesn't go beyond topless and G-strings. Although designed for men, the show contains little to make women or couples uncomfortable. VIP seating includes a line pass.

Danny Gans: "The Man of Many Voices"

Type of Show: Impressions and variety

Host Casino and Showroom: Rio—Copacabana Entertainment Complex until January 2000. In April 2000 Gans moves to the Mirage.

Reservations and Information: (800) 456-4564 for the Mirage; or (800) PLAY-RIO for the Rio

Admission with Taxes: $83, includes tax, 2 drinks, and gratuity

Cast Size: About 4

Nights of Lowest Attendance: Thursday

Usual Show Times: 8 p.m.   *Dark:* Monday and Tuesday

Topless: No

Author's Rating: ★★★★

Overall Appeal by Age:

Under 21	21–37	38–50	51 and older
★★★★	★★★★	★★★★	★★★★

Duration: Hour and 25 minutes

Comments   Danny Gans is a monster talent. He does more than a hundred impressions during the show, among them Michael Jackson, Willie Nelson, James Stewart, Kermit the Frog, and President Clinton. His comedy is cerebral, sophisticated, and hilarious, making this perhaps the most intelligent show in town.

Consumer Tips   The Rio showroom is one of the city's best designed. Some seats are far from the stage, but sightlines are excellent. The sound system is awesome. The Mirage has built a new state-of-the-art theater expressly for Gans. However, as good as this show is, the $83 ticket price is more than Gans is worth. After Gans' departure, former Partridge Family member David Cassidy will headline at the Rio.

EFX!

Type of Show: Grand-scale musical production show

Host Casino and Showroom: MGM Grand—Grand Theater

Reservations and Information: 891-7777 or (800) 929-1111

Admission with Taxes: $57.50 general admission; $72 preferred admission; children (ages 12 and younger) $35

Cast Size: 70

Nights of Lowest Attendance: Tuesday, Wednesday

Usual Show Times: 7:30 and 10:30 p.m.

Dark: Sunday and Monday

Topless: No

Author's Rating: ★★★★½

Overall Appeal by Age:

Under 21	21–37	38–50	51 and older
★★★	★★★★½	★★★★½	★★★★

Duration: Hour and a half

Comments   EFX! (pronounced "Effects") is designed to overwhelm. Tommy Tune recently joined the cast of 70, and he is excellent. Taking several roles, he guides the audience through a robotic and technological odyssey in time and space.

We were surprised by how beautiful and aesthetically grounded *EFX!* is, and also by its delightful humor. This stunning show makes excellent use of its technology rather than numbing the audience with special effects. Although the name is stupid and misleading, *EFX!* is a must-see, second only to *Cirque du Soleil's Mystere* as the city's best production show.

Consumer Tips   EFX! technology is so complex that malfunctions have been common. The only bad seats are those right up front where fake fog periodically envelops them. The better seats are about four tiers from the front and in the center. Allow an extra 20–30 minutes with either valet or self-parking.

Enter the Night

Type of Show: Music, dance, and variety production show

Host Casino and Showroom: Stardust—Stardust Theatre

Reservations and Information: 732-6328 or (800) 824-6033

Admission with Taxes: $30 general seating; $35 premium; $45 executive booth (includes 2 drinks and gratuity)

Cast Size: About 72

Nights of Lowest Attendance: Thursday, Sunday

Usual Show Times: 7:30 and 10:30 p.m., Tuesday–Thursday, Saturday; 8 p.m., Sunday and Monday   *Dark:* Friday

Topless: Yes

Author's Rating: ★★★★

Overall Appeal by Age:

Under 21	21–37	38–50	51 and older
N/A	★★★½	★★★★	★★★★

Duration: Hour and a half

Comments   Modern yet timeless, sophisticated and elegant. The production draws upon night's mystery, reverie, sultriness, and eroticism to provide sequences of dance and music. Specialty acts are blended gracefully. In the most beautiful sequence, dancers move among laser patterns. Costumes are possibly the best designed in Las Vegas.

The show might seem slow to some and may not offer enough variety for others, but it remains unique in beauty and tone.

Consumer Tips   Those older than 40 will most appreciate *Enter the Night.* Younger than 21 not admitted. Allow extra time to reach the showroom if you self-park.

An Evening at La Cage

Type of Show: Female-impersonator revue

Host Casino and Showroom: Riviera—Mardi Gras Showrooms, third floor

Reservations and Information: 794-9433 or (800) 634-3420

Admission with Taxes: $27 general admission; $35 VIP (includes 2 drinks and gratuity)

Cast Size: About 20

Nights of Lowest Attendance: Sunday, Monday

Usual Show Times: 7:30 and 9:30 p.m., with an 11:15 p.m. show Wednesdays   *Dark:* Tuesday

Topless: No

Author's Rating: ★★★

Overall Appeal by Age:

Under 21	21–37	38–50	51 and older
N/A	★★★½	★★★	★★★

Duration: Hour and 15 minutes

Comments A high-tempo show with a great sense of humor, *La Cage* is outrageous, lusty, weird, and sensitive. Celebrities impersonated include Joan Rivers, Tina Turner, Cher, and Carol Channing. Dancers also are men impersonating women. Some impersonators are convincing. Others look like what they are: men in drag.

Consumer Tips Three shows—*Riviera Comedy Club, Crazy Girls,* and *La Cage*—play the Mardi Gras Showrooms. In addition, *Splash* is in the Versailles Theater. If you want to see several in a night, allow at least an hour and a half between performances. Show-buffet tickets are a good value.

Seating is by maître d'. Once seated, you fetch your drinks (your ticket stub is the voucher).

Folies Bergere (The Best of)

Type of Show: Music, dance, and variety-production show

Host Casino and Showroom: Tropicana—Tiffany Theater

Reservations and Information: 739-2411 or (800) 634-4000

Admission with Taxes: $50–60

Cast Size: About 90

Nights of Lowest Attendance: Monday, Tuesday, Sunday

Usual Show Times: 8 and 10:30 p.m.

Dark: Thursday

Topless: Yes

Author's Rating: ★★★

Overall Appeal by Age:

Under 21	21–37	38–50	51 and older
★★	★★★	★★★	★★★★

Duration: Hour and a half

Comments   This classy dance and musical production modeled on the bawdy Parisian revue of the same name has played the Tropicana intermittently since 1959. You get what you expect: exotically clad (or unclad) showgirls and cancan dancers, chorus lines, singers, and music with a turn-of-the-century French cabaret feel. A talented cast slogs through a dated format.

Consumer Tips   More booth seating than in most showrooms; almost every seat has a good view. Buffet-show package is $13 more. Tickets don't include drinks. Rest rooms are distant. All seats are reserved.

Forever Plaid

Type of Show: '50s musical nostalgia

Host Casino and Showroom: Flamingo—Bugsy's Theater

Reservations and Information: 733-3333 or (800) 221-7299

Admission with Taxes: $25

Cast Size: 6

Nights of Lowest Attendance: Wednesday, Thursday

Usual Show Times: 7:30 and 10 p.m.

Dark: Monday

Topless: No

Author's Rating: ★★★½

Overall Appeal by Age:

Under 21	21–37	38–50	51 and older
★★	★★★	★★★½	★★★★

Duration: Hour and a half

Comments   A quirky, clever, small-stage revue, *Forever Plaid* is the story of a quartet modeled on the guy groups popular in the late '50s and early '60s. The Four Plaids die in a car crash en route to their first big gig, then 20 years later return to life to perform that concert.

The show is held together by song and dance, clever shtick, and engaging characterizations. But it's the music that has earned *Forever Plaid* its rave reviews. The Plaids do all or part of 30 golden favorites.

If you don't want to be hauled on stage to play the top piano part of "Heart and Soul," don't sit up front.

Consumer Tips Maître d' seating. Drinks are extra ($2–3.50); carry a fresh one from the casino.

The Great Radio City Spectacular

Type of Show: Broadway-oriented musical variety show

Host Casino and Showroom: Flamingo Hilton—Flamingo Show-room

Reservations and Information: 733-3333 or (800) 221-7299

Admission with Taxes: $54–67 dinner; $38–47 cocktail

Cast Size: About 30

Nights of Lowest Attendance: Wednesday, Thursday

Usual Show Times: 7:45 and 10:30 p.m., Saturday and Monday; 8 p.m., Sunday–Thursday

Dark: Friday

Topless: No

Author's Rating: ★★★½

Overall Appeal by Age:

Under 21	21–37	38–50	51 and older
N/A	★★★½	★★★★	★★★★

Duration: Hour and a half

Comments How many variations can a line of high-kicking cho-rus girls achieve? Quite a few, the Radio City Music Hall Rock-ettes prove. Aided competently by four male dancers, the stat-uesque Rockettes stay crisp and fresh as they range from tap to cancan to a typical Las Vegas finale.

Alternating as master of ceremonies and lead vocalist are Paige O'Hara (vocal star of *Beauty and the Beast*) and Susan Anton. While almost devoid of surprises, the show is fast-paced and main-tains excellent continuity.

Consumer Tips Maître d' seating. Dinner or cocktail early show. Dinner ($7 to $20 extra) seats at 5:45 p.m. Cocktail seating (two drinks) is at 7:15 p.m. Late show has cocktails only; seating be-gins around 9:45 p.m.

Imagine

Type of Show: Musical/circus production show

Host Casino and Showroom: Luxor—Luxor Theatre

Reservations and Information: 262-4400

Admission with Taxes: $40

Cast Size: 45

Nights of Lowest Attendance: Sunday

Usual Show Times: 7:30 and 10 p.m.   *Dark:* Thursday

Topless: No

Author's Rating: ★★★½

Overall Appeal by Age:

Under 21	21–37	38–50	51 and Older
★★★★	★★★½	★★★½	★★★½

Duration: Hour and 20 minutes

Comments   Like *Cirque du Soleil, Imagine* weaves acrobatics, juggling, clowning, and other circus skills. It's a big show performed by a talented cast, but it isn't in the same league as *Cirque*. Still, if you've never seen *Cirque* and don't want to pay $70 to do so, *Imagine* is an entertaining, less expensive substitute.

Consumer Tips   Luxor Theatre is one of the city's best show venues. All seats are reserved. Drinks aren't included; a cash bar is outside the showroom.

Jubilee!

Type of Show: Grand-scale musical and variety production show

Host Casino and Showroom: Bally's—The Jubilee Theater

Reservations and Information: 967-4567 or (800) 237-SHOW

Admission with Taxes: $49.50–66 ($2.50 extra on credit card purchase)

Cast Size: 100

Nights of Lowest Attendance: Sunday, Monday

Usual Show Times: 7:30 and 10:30 p.m., Monday, Wednesday, Thursday, and Saturday; 7:30 p.m., Sunday and Tuesday

Dark: Friday

Topless: Yes

Author's Rating: ★★★★

Overall Appeal by Age:

Under 21	21–37	38–50	51 and older
★★★	★★★	★★★½	★★★★

Duration: Hour and 58 minutes

Comments *Jubilee!* is the quintessential Las Vegas production show, faithfully following a successful decades-old formula: elaborate musical numbers, extravagant sets, beautiful topless showgirls, and quality variety acts. The show is lavish, sexy, and well-performed, but redundant to the point of numbing.

Two highlights are the awe-inspiring telling of the Samson and Delilah saga, and the story of the *Titanic,* from launch to sinking. The spectacle is incredible.

Consumer Tips Seating is at banquet tables at the foot of the stage ($60; too close and cramped), one row of booths above the tables ($66 and worth it); and 789 theater-style seats ($55 in the middle of the room, $49.50 at back). Table and booth seats get cocktail service; theater-seat patrons carry in their drinks.

Lance Burton: Master Magician

Type of Show: Magical illusion with dancing and specialty acts

Host Casino and Showroom: Monte Carlo—Lance Burton Theatre

Reservations and Information: 730-7000 or (800) 311-8999

Admission with Taxes: $37 balcony seating; $42 main-floor seating

Cast Size: 14

Nights of Lowest Attendance: Thursday, Friday

Usual Show Times: 7:30 and 10:30 p.m.   *Dark:* Sunday, Monday

Topless: No

Author's Rating: ★★★★

Overall Appeal by Age:

Under 21	21–37	38–50	51 and older
★★★★	★★★★	★★★★	★★★★

Duration: Hour and a half

Comments Lance Burton's is one of only two of the city's magic shows that escape the curse of redundancy. He performs in tight-fitting clothing (nothing can be concealed) and displays sleight of hand not seen in other showrooms.

Consumer Tips It's hard to appreciate Burton's subtle moves if you're in the boonies or balcony. Try to sit on the main floor near the stage. Drinks cost extra.

Legends in Concert

Type of Show: Celebrity-impersonator musical production show

Host Casino and Showroom: Imperial Palace—Imperial Theatre

Reservations and Information: 794-3261

Admission with Taxes: $34.50 adults (includes tax, 2 drinks, and gratuity); $19.50 children (ages 12 and under)

Cast Size: About 20

Nights of Lowest Attendance: Wednesday, Thursday

Usual Show Times: 7:30 and 10:30 p.m.   *Dark:* Sunday

Topless: No

Author's Rating: ★★★★

Overall Appeal by Age:

Under 21	21–37	38–50	51 and older
★★★★	★★★★	★★★★	★★★★

Duration: Hour and a half

Comments   A highly talented cast of impersonators re-creates musical performances by celebrities including Elvis, Richie Valens, Cher, the Four Tops, and Gloria Estefan. Likenesses are remarkable. Impersonators sing and/or play their own instruments. The upbeat show is possibly the fastest-moving in town.

Consumer Tips   *Legends* almost always plays to a full house on weekends; reserve early. Maître d' seating; arrive 40 minutes before show time. If you self-park, allow extra time.

Michael Flatley's Lord of the Dance

Type of Show: Celtic music and dance production

Host Casino and Showroom: New York–New York—Broadway Theater

Reservations and Information: 740-6815

Admission with Taxes: $50 Tuesday–Thursday; $60 Friday and Saturday

Cast Size: 44

Nights of Lowest Attendance: Wednesday

Usual Show Times: 7:30 and 10 p.m., Tuesday, Wednesday, and Saturday; 9 p.m., Thursday and Friday

Dark: Sunday and Monday

Special Comments: Michael Flatley does not dance

Topless: No

Author's Rating: ★★★★ (Rollicking fun)

Overall Appeal by Age:

Under 21	21–37	38–50	51 and older
★★★★	★★★★	★★★★	★★★★

Duration of Presentation: Hour and a half

Comments   Michael Flatley, once the male star of *Riverdance,* left the company and opened *Lord of the Dance* in Dublin in 1996. Since that time the two productions have been fierce competitors. With its jubilant score, relentless pace, and exacting precision, *Lord of the Dance* is decidedly an upper—an evening's entertainment that leaves you curiously both energized and drained. While there's great subtlety and delicacy in the show, it is when the entire cast of dancers is on stage at once with 80 feet thundering in flawless unison that *Lord of the Dance* realizes its potential. We like *Lord of the Dance* and think you will too. It's not the typical Las Vegas show, but it is a mainline dose of Celtic music and dance. Believe us, that's enough.

Consumer Tips   If you've seen a live performance of *Riverdance, Lord of the Dance* is essentially more of the same. If you've seen *Riverdance* only on video and liked it, we heartily recommend *Lord of the Dance.* The live production (of either show) has an impact that can only be imagined by watching a video. *Lord of the Dance* sells out most nights, so purchase your tickets by phone with a credit card before leaving home. Try to get seats somewhere in the middle of the theater—you want to be at least 20 rows back from the stage.

Siegfried & Roy

Type of Show: Production magic and illusion show with choreography and great spectacle

Host Casino and Showroom: Mirage—Siegfried & Roy Theatre

Reservations and Information: 792-7777 or (800) 456-4564

Admission with Taxes: $90 (includes 2 drinks, all gratuities, and souvenir program)

Cast Size: About 88

Nights of Lowest Attendance: Sunday, Monday

Usual Show Times: 7:30 and 11 p.m.   *Dark:* Wednesday and Thursday

Topless: No

Author's Rating: ★★★★

Overall Appeal by Age:

Under 21	21–37	38–50	51 and older
★★★★★	★★★★★	★★★★★	★★★★★

Duration: Hour and 40 minutes

Comments   This show revolutionized Las Vegas production shows, paving the way for *Cirque du Soleil's Mystere* and *"O," EFX!*, and *Chicago*. But *Siegfried & Roy* delivers a great deal more than magic and illusion. Sets and special effects are extraordinary, even overwhelming. But the presentation remains tasteful and sophisticated.

A fantasy depicting good and evil provides a backdrop for illusions by Siegfried and Roy. These involve (among other things) white tigers, elephants, and mechanical dragons. At the show's end, Siegfried and Roy appear as themselves and spotlight their famous white tigers.

If there's a problem with *Siegfried & Roy,* it's the one plaguing most magic-illusion shows: redundancy. How many ways can something in a box disappear before the illusion loses its impact? Does it matter that the boxes and animals keep getting larger?

We recommend *Siegfried & Roy* as a landmark Las Vegas show. The question is whether it's worth the $90 admission. The high quality of competing shows priced $18–20 less suggests that *Siegfried & Roy* is significantly overpriced.

Consumer Tips   Even at $90 a pop, the show sells out almost every night. Seats are reserved by computer, but patrons have some say in location. Visibility is good from all seats.

To see *Siegfried & Roy* on short notice, try for the late show

Sunday, Monday, or Tuesday. Contact the box office between 2:30 and 5 p.m. A riskier, same-day strategy is to try the box office a half-hour before show time. Among 1,500 seats are almost always a few cancellations or no-shows.

Hotel guests can charge tickets to their room. If they're unclaimed, the guest still must pay.

Because all seats are reserved, don't tip the maître d' or captain. We recommend entering the theater 25 to 30 minutes before show time. If you self-park, allow an extra 10 to 15 minutes to reach the showroom.

If you enjoy magic but are unwilling to pay $90 for *Siegfried & Roy,* try *David Copperfield* or *Lance Burton.* They lack the elaborate productions, but these magicians perform comparable, if not superior, illusions, and with less redundancy. Also consider *Spellbound* at Harrah's.

Spellbound

Type of Show: Musical production show with emphasis on magic

Host Casino and Showroom: Harrah's—Commander's Theatre

Reservations and Information: 369-5111 or (800) 392-9002

Admission with Taxes: $40 (includes tax, tip, and 1 drink)

Cast Size: About 25

Nights of Lowest Attendance: Thursday

Usual Show Times: 7:30 and 10 p.m.

Dark: Sunday

Topless: No

Author's Rating: ★★★1/2

Overall Appeal by Age:

Under 21	21–37	38–50	51 and older
★★★½	★★★½	★★★½	★★★½

Duration: Hour and 20 minutes

Comments One of the city's most beautiful, comfortable showrooms. The show is sensual without nudity and tastefully produced. It features first-rate magic plus energetic street dance, gymnastics, and imaginative lighting and laser effects. *Spellbound* is solid but doesn't break any new ground.

Consumer Tips Children 5 or older pay the adult price.

Splash

Type of Show: Musical variety-aquacade show

Host Casino and Showroom: Riviera—Versailles Theater

Reservations and Information: 794-9301 or (800) 634-3420

Admission with Taxes: $57 VIP; $46 general

Cast Size: About 50

Nights of Lowest Attendance: Sunday, Tuesday, Wednesday

Usual Show Times: Daily, 7:30 and 10:30 p.m.

Topless: Late show only

Author's Rating: ★★★

Overall Appeal by Age:

Under 21	21–37	38–50	51 and older
★★★	★★★½	★★★½	★★★

Duration: Hour and a half

Comments   A thread-thin plot holds *Splash* together: A super submarine visits the North Pole, Bermuda Triangle, and Atlantis. On its journey, the sub stops at so many ports—four rip-roaring production numbers and a dozen gimmicks and variety acts—that you wonder if anyone is steering the thing. One performance stands out: a break dancing and gangsta segment by the four Dragon Masters. When the journey ends, a few audience members seem disoriented, but most got exactly what they expected from a Las Vegas extravaganza.

Consumer Tips   All seats are assigned in the order in which reservations are received; the earlier you buy, the better your seats. The VIP section has replaced most banquet tables, and everyone has an unobstructed view.

Admission doesn't include drinks. Glassware isn't allowed; bring your beverages in plastic cups. Meal deals at the Riviera's Mardi Gras Food Court are often available; check visitor magazines for coupons.

Steve Wyrick, World-Class Magician

Type of Show: Magic and illusion production show

Host Casino and Showroom: Lady Luck—Lady Luck Theatre

Reservations and Information: 385-4386 after 4:30 p.m. PST

Admission with Taxes: $33

Cast Size: About 10

Nights of Lowest Attendance: Wednesday

Usual Show Times: Tuesday–Sunday, 7:30 and 10:30 p.m.
   Dark: Monday

Topless: No

Author's Rating: ★★★★

Overall Appeal by Age:

Under 21	21–37	38–50	51 and older
★★★★	★★★★	★★★★	★★★★

Duration: Hour and 20 minutes

Comments   This is the show scene's version of "we try harder." Wyrick digs deep and delivers some great illusion and sleight of hand. His style and presentation are reminiscent of Lance Burton, but each illusion has a unique twist.

Consumer Tips   The theater has a few bad seats. You can usually swap just before show time. There's a cash bar with table service.

Tournament of Kings

Type of Show: Jousting and medieval pageant

Host Casino and Showroom: Excalibur—King Arthur's Arena

Reservations and Information: 597-7600 or (800) 637-8133

Admission with Taxes: $41 includes dinner and gratuity

Cast Size: 35 (with 38 horses)

Nights of Lowest Attendance: Monday and Tuesday

Usual Show Times: 6 and 8:30 p.m.

Topless: No

Author's Rating: ★★★

Overall Appeal by Age Group:

Under 21	21–37	38–50	51 and older
★★★★	★★★★	★★★★	★★★★

Duration: Hour and a half

Comments   *Tournament of Kings* is a retooled version of *King Arthur's Tournament.* It's basically the same show, with a slightly different plot twist. Arthur summons the kings of eight European countries to a sporting competition in honor of his son Christopher. Guests view the arena from dinner tables divided into sections; a king is designated to represent each section in the competition.

Soup is served to the strains of the opening march. The kings enter on horseback. Precisely when the King of Hungary is introduced, dinner arrives. The kings engage in contests with flags, dummy heads, javelins, swords, maces, and shields and joust a while, too. The horsework, fighting, and especially the jousting are exciting, and the music and sound effects are well executed.

Right on cue, Mordred the Evil One crashes the party, accompanied by his Dragon Enforcers. Arthur is mortally wounded and all the kings are knocked out, leaving Christopher to battle the forces of evil and emerge—surprise!—victorious in the end. But it's not over. The coronation is the culmination, after some acrobatics and human-tower stunts from a specialty act. Finally, the handsome new king goes out in a (literal) blaze of glory.

Consumer Tips   One of the few Las Vegas shows suitable for the whole family, and one of the fewer dinner shows, *Tournament of Kings* enjoys great popularity and often plays to a full house. Reserved seats can be purchased with a credit card up to six days in advance by calling the number listed above (extra $2 charge if you order by phone). Or you can show up at the Excalibur box office, which opens at 8 a.m., up to six days ahead.

No matter where you sit, you're close to the action. Consider bringing a wrap. Seating is reserved, so you can walk in at the last minute and don't have to tip any greeters or seaters.

Dinner is served without utensils and eaten with the hands, so you might want to wash up beforehand. You might consider bringing some aluminum foil and a bag to take out leftovers. Beverage is limited to soda with dinner, but water and cocktails are available. Service is adequate; no one tips, so you'll be a hero if you do.

Comedy Clubs

Stand-up comedy abounds in Las Vegas. Several production shows feature comedians, and at least one comedy headliner (Jerry Seinfeld, Rodney Dangerfield, Joan Rivers, etc.) is usually playing in town. Finally, there are the comedy clubs.

These are smaller showrooms with simple stages and two to five stand-up comics. In most, each week brings a new show. There are five bona fide Las Vegas comedy clubs:

MGM Grand	*Catch a Rising Star*
Harrah's	*An Evening at the Improv*
Maxim	*Comedy Max*
Riviera	*Comedy Club*
Tropicana	*Comedy Stop*

Comedy clubs are never dark. There are two shows each night, seven days a week (except at the Riviera, which offers three performances nightly). The humor and the audience tend to be young and irreverent. Comedy clubs' affordable entertainment is very popular with both locals and tourists.

Comedians perform sequentially; what you get depends on who is performing. Humor ranges from slapstick to obscene. Some comics are better than others, but all are solid.

Catch a Rising Star

Type of Show: Stand-up comedy
Host Casino and Showroom: MGM Grand—Center Stage Cabaret
Reservations and Information: 891-7777
Admission with Taxes: $16–18
Cast Size: 2 to 4 comedians
Nights of Lowest Attendance: Sunday, Monday
Usual Show Times: Daily, 8 and 10:30 p.m.

Comments Maître d' seating. Drinks aren't included; buy from a server at your table. Reservations by phone with credit card carry a $2 service charge per ticket. Valet or self-parking, allow 15 minutes extra to reach the showroom.

Comedy Max

Type of Show: Stand-up comedy
Host Casino and Showroom: Maxim—Cabaret Showroom
Reservations and Information: 731-4300 or (800) 634-6787
Admission with Taxes: $18.75 includes tax and 2 drinks
Cast Size: Usually 3 comedians

Nights of Lowest Attendance: Wednesday, Thursday
Usual Show Times: Daily, 7 and 9 p.m.

Comments   Show/buffet combo is $21.95. Maître d' seating; exchange ticket stubs for two drinks brought by waiter. Visibility good from most seats. Park in the Maxim's garage on Flamingo.

Comedy Stop

Type of Show: Stand-up comedy
Host Casino and Showroom: Tropicana—Comedy Stop Showroom
Reservations and Information: 739-2714
Admission with Taxes: $16 with 2 drinks and gratuity
Cast Size: Usually 3 comedians
Nights of Lowest Attendance: Monday–Wednesday
Usual Show Times: Daily, 8 and 10:30 p.m.
Duration: Hour and a half

Comments   Reach the showroom via the elevator between the main casino and shopping arcade. Maître d' seating, all at banquet tables. Exchange ticket stubs for two drinks at self-service bar. If you self-park, allow 10 extra minutes.

An Evening at the Improv

Type of Show: Stand-up comedy
Host Casino and Showroom: Harrah's—The Improv
Reservations and Information: 369-5111
Admission with Taxes: $17
Cast Size: 3 to 4 comedians
Nights of Lowest Attendance: Wednesday, Thursday
Usual Show Times: Daily, 8 and 10:30 p.m.   *Dark:* Monday

Comments   Cash bar. Showroom is on second floor; use escalator from casino.

Riviera Comedy Club

Type of Show: Stand-up comedy
Host Casino and Showroom: Riviera—Mardi Gras Showrooms, second floor
Reservations and Information: 794-9433

Admission with Taxes: $19 general admission; $25 VIP (includes tax, tip, and 2 drinks)

Cast Size: About 4

Nights of Lowest Attendance: Sunday–Wednesday

Usual Show Times: 8, 10, and Friday and Saturday only at 11:45 p.m.

Comments   Show-buffet tickets are good value. Maître d' seating. Self-service bar; ticket stub is your voucher.

Las Vegas Nightlife

With the exception of patronizing comedy clubs, locals stay away from the Strip. Visitors, conversely, almost never leave it. Both groups miss some great night life.

Lounges and clubs are friendly citywide. Visitors can feel comfortable in places primarily frequented by locals, and vice versa. Profiled here alphabetically are the better nightspots.

Microbreweries, described in Part Five, Dining and Restaurants, are another off-Strip option.

THE BEACH

Dance music of the '70s, '80s, and '90s
Who Goes There: 21–40; locals, visitors, conventioneers

365 Convention Center (Paradise intersection, across from the Convention Center); 731-1925
Strip Zone 1

Comments: "Local's favorite" party club. Long lines from 9 p.m. past 2 a.m.on weekends. Garage is reserved for valet on weekends; park across the street at the convention center. Smoke can be heavy. Women alone can expect to find company.

CLUB PARADISE

Upscale topless bar
Who Goes There: Men 21–65; professionals and conventioneers

4416 Paradise Road; 734-7990
Strip Zone 1

Comments: Very plush. More than 100 dancers. VIP section ($100 minimum per person, plus cover charge) has its own stage. Valet parking only. Maître d' seating. A gentleman's club, but women are welcome.

CLUB RIO

Nightclub—Top 40 music
Who Goes There: 25–35 professionals; locals and visitors

3700 W. Flamingo Road (Rio Hotel); 252-7777
Strip Zone 1

Comments: Hottest nightclub for successful singles and the chic well-to-do. Spacious dance floor. Music loud but not deafening. Long lines after 11 p.m. Jackets for men, dresses for women. Watch your step on terraced levels as you access dance floor.

DRINK AND EAT TOO

Top 40 blended with taped '70s and '80s music
Who Goes There: 25–40; locals, visitors, and college students

Corner of Harmon and Kovall; 796-5519
Strip Zone 1

Comments: Guys act cool smoking long cigars; gals act like the guys don't impress them. Enclosed courtyard is main dance floor. Arrive well before midnight to avoid lines and parking congestion. Dress to impress.

DYLAN'S SALOON & DANCE HALL

Recorded country music
Who Goes There: 25–50; urban and rodeo cowboys

4660 S. Boulder Highway; 451-4006
Southeast Zone 5

Comments: Two-stepping and pool shooting. Recently voted best country bar. Odors of beer and cigarettes thick. On busy nights, party flows into fenced, flood-lit, dirt area adjacent to parking lot. Some parking areas quite dark; women should request an escort.

FINAL SCORE SPORTS BAR

Sports bar
Who Goes There: 21–35; locals, Air Force personnel,
college crowd, visitors

5111 Boulder Highway (Sam's Town Hotel & Gambling Hall); 456-7777
Southeast Zone 5

Comments: Indoor basketball and outdoor volleyball, plus pool, electronic darts. Friday and Saturday nights busiest. Good food. Use valet parking.

GILLEY'S SALOON, DANCE HALL, AND BARBECUE

Live country and rock and roll
Who Goes There: 21–55; real and urban cowboys, locals and tourists

3120 Las Vegas Boulevard, South (New Frontier); 794-8200
Strip Zone 1

Comments: The band plays two-minute country tunes during dinner sets, then cranks up the tempo later. The dance floor gets crowded with two-steppers and line dancers, while patrons take turns on the free but ferocious hydraulic bull. The atmosphere is as heavily country as anywhere else in town, certainly the heaviest on the Strip. The price is right no matter what mood you're in, but it helps to either be in, or ready for, cowboy hats, silver buckles, and fringed blouses. The joint is sedate until late.

THE NIGHTCLUB

Top 40/show combination
Who Goes There: 30–50; visitors, locals, convention-goers/
business people

3000 Paradise Road (Las Vegas Hilton); 732-5755 or 732-5422
Strip Zone 1

Comments: Trendy art deco hot spot. No-pressure environment.
Good live renditions of pop music; small dance floor. Arrive early
for choice seating. Parking areas distant; take a cab or use valet.

OLYMPIC GARDEN

Topless bar
Who Goes There: Men 21–65; locals, visitors, and conventioneers

1531 Las Vegas Boulevard, South; 385-8987
Strip Zone 1

Comments: Connoisseurs consider this the city's finest topless
joint. It's not the classiest club, but it's one of the least aggressive,
and women are top-of-the-line. Male strippers perform weekends
(men must be accompanied by a woman to watch). Large, well-
lit parking lot.

ORBIT

Dance
Who Goes There: 21–29; college students, Generation Xers

4455 Paradise Road (Hard Rock Hotel); 693-5000
Strip Zone 1

Comments: Male and female go-go dancers gyrate on stage as
young, hip crowd fills the dance floor. Two bars are jammed. Parking is limited on busy nights; use valet or take a cab.

PALOMINO CLUB

Totally nude dance club
Who Goes There: Men 21–65; tourists, locals, conventioneers

1848 Las Vegas Boulevard, North; 642-2984
North Las Vegas Zone 4

Comments: About nine professionals and as many so-called amateurs strip completely each night. A stand-up comic spells the dancers. Lighted self-parking. Maître d' seating. Pay the cover, order two drinks, and stay all night if you behave. Women welcome.

PEPPERMILL INN'S FIRESIDE LOUNGE

Romantic and quiet
Who Goes There: 25–50; locals and tourists

2985 Las Vegas Boulevard, South; 735-4177 (Restaurant),
735-7635 (Lounge)
Strip Zone 1

Comments: Longtime local favorite. An inviting, tranquil lounge unexpectly situated in a 24-hour coffee shop. Soft rock and pop play. Drinks are pricey, and quality varies. Service is relaxed. If you really need to unwind, order your first drink from the bartender.

RA

Top 40, techno, and dance
Who Goes There: 21–35; locals and tourists, college students to professionals

---

3900 Las Vegas Boulevard, South (Luxor); (702) 262-4000
Strip Zone 1

Comments: Egyptian-themed nightclub. Singles line the railing to watch the dance floor. Go-go dancers lead the throng. Cigar afficionados occupy one of two lounges. Use valet parking. Arrive early or be prepared to wait (hotel guests use the VIP line).

SAM'S TOWN DANCE HALL

DJ country-western music
Who Goes There: 25–40 weekends, 25–60 during the week; locals, tourists, cowboys

5111 Boulder Highway (Sam's Town Hotel); 456-7777
Southeast Zone 5

Comments: Country music handled by a deejay. Free line and swing-dance lessons. The party starts at 9 p.m. Monday through Saturday. Sundays and Mondays include karaoke. Dance hall gets quite smoky. Music is loud; talk outside. Women can expect to be asked to dance. Park in the "Nellis parking barn" connected to the casino.

SAND DOLLAR BLUES LOUNGE

Rhythm and blues
Who Goes There: Bikers to yuppies

3355 Spring Mountain Road (at Polaris); 871-6651
Southwest Zone 3

Comments: Marvelous blues. Standing-room only on Friday, Saturday, and special-event nights. Club's unshaven appearance may deter some solo ladies, but regulars make sure everything stays cool. Lounge is smoky. Club is hard to spot at night; arrive early or by cab.

STUDIO 54

Dance, Top 40
Who Goes There: 25–40; locals, tourists, and trendy people

3799 Las Vegas Boulevard, South (MGM Grand); 891-1111
Strip Zone 1

Comments: New York club that set the standard for disco in the '70s comes to Las Vegas. If you love a club with attitude, this is your place. If you prefer fun and friendliness, try RA or Club Rio. Entrance is distant from valet and self-parking.

TOMMY ROCKER'S CANTINA AND CAFE

Top 40 and Jimmy Buffett–style music
Who Goes There: 25–30; professionals and career starters

4275 S. Industrial Road; 261-6688
Strip Zone 1

Comments: Voted best live-music club in local survey. Owner and musician Tommy Rocker plays when he's in town. Ample parking. Music loud, not deafening. Arrive early for best seating.

VOODOO CAFE AND LOUNGE

Restaurant and lounge with live entertainment
Who Goes There: 25+; upscale visitors and locals

3700 W. Flamingo Road (Rio Hotel); 257-7777, ext. 8090
Southwest Zone 3

Comments: The 50th-floor restaurant and 51st-floor lounge (smoky) are surrounded by glass windows, connected by stairs. Patio offers electrifying view of Strip but may be closed by weather. Jazz and blues in lounge. After 10 p.m. Friday and Saturday, lines are long at VooDoo elevators (managed by a humorless staff). Park in "Masquerade Village" garage. Want to dance? Go to Club Rio.

Las Vegas below the Belt

DON'T WORRY, BE HAPPY

Las Vegas exults in its permissiveness and makes every effort to give visitors freedom to have fun. Behind the hedonism, however, is a police department that works hard to make Las Vegas safe for visitors. In few other large cities could travelers carry large sums of money safely. The Strip and downtown, especially, are well patrolled, and most hotels have in-house security forces.

Police patrol downtown and the Strip in cars, on foot, and on mountain bikes, which allow quick pursuit of pickpockets or purse snatchers. Streets connecting the Strip with Paradise Road and the

Las Vegas Convention Center are also safe. When tourists are robbed, they're usually far from downtown or the Strip, and often are trying to buy drugs.

ORGANIZED CRIME AND CHEATING

Few visitors walk through a casino without wondering if the games are rigged or the place is owned by the mob. When legalized gambling was new, few people outside of organized crime had experience managing gaming operations. Hence, mob figures came to work in Nevada.

The formation of the Nevada Gaming Commission and the State Gaming Control Board as part of a government assault on organized crime purged the mob from Las Vegas. This ouster, plus the Nevada Corporate Gaming Acts of 1967 and 1969 (allowing publicly held corporations such as Hilton, Holiday Inn, Bally, and MGM to own casinos), at last brought respectability to Las Vegas gambling.

The limited cheating that exists in Las Vegas is usually perpetrated by gamblers, not the house, though honest players at the cheater's table may also get burned.

Skin Games—Sex in Las Vegas   Although nudity, prostitution, and pornography are tightly regulated in Las Vegas, the city offers a near-perfect environment for marketing sex. Over 50% of visitors are men, most between ages 21 and 59. Some come to party, and many, particularly convention-goers, are lonely. Almost all have time and money on their hands.

Stripping on the Strip   Las Vegas is moving moving away from nudity and eroticism. "Girlie" (and "boy") shows are tame by many standards. In larger showrooms, this is an accommodation to the growing percentage of women in the audience. More often, however, it's the result of a city law that says you can offer totally nude entertainment or you can serve alcoholic beverages, not both.

Topless showgirls often merely embellish a production that features song, dance, and variety acts. Some shows offer both a topless and a "covered" performance.

Topless Bars   The main difference between a topless bar and a totally nude nightclub (aside from the alcohol regulations) is a Gstring. Topless bars aren't inexpensive, but they're conveniently located, including Girls of Glitter Gulch on Fremont Street and Cheetah's at 2112 Western Ave. We profile Palomino Club, Club Paradise, and Olympic Garden (pages 118–21).

How Felons Choose Their Victims

Felons choose their marks by observing a potential victim's attire and behavior. Wearing lots of jewelry and flaunting big bills are sure to attract attention. Stupid bets suggest inexperience, and excessive drinking lowers inhibitions and defenses. Playing without friends suggests you're a solitary business traveler or on vacation and perhaps hungry for companionship.

Beware of loners of either sex. If you meet somebody interesting, resist the urge to rush the relationship. Don't go anywhere to be alone. Don't tell anyone your room number. If you're traveling alone, don't say so.

Part Three

Gambling

The Way It Is

Gambling is the reason Las Vegas exists. It fuels the local economy, paves the roads, and gives the city its identity.

To tourists, gambling is a game. To those who earn their living from it, gambling is mathematics. The gambler *hopes* to win a fortune, but the casinos *know* that in the long run the fortune will belong to the house. The games, the odds, and the payoffs are carefully designed to ensure that outcome.

The casino does risk one bet: that it can entice enough people to play.

A casino costs millions of dollars, with a staff numbering in the hundreds. Before a nickel of profit is set aside, all the bills must be paid and the payroll met. Regardless of the house's overwhelming advantage at the tables, it cannot stay in business unless a lot of people come to play, and the larger the casino, the more gamblers are required.

Casinos compete aggressively and creatively to lure customers, offering low-cost buffets, dollar shrimp cocktails, stage shows, lounge entertainment, free drinks, gambling tournaments, and slot clubs. The most recent tactic is to package the casino itself as a tourist attraction. This explains the Mirage's erupting volcano in the front yard, white tigers in the entrance hall, and live sharks in the parlor.

The Short Run

If you ask a mathematician or a casino owner if you can win gambling in a casino, the truthful answer is yes, but only in the short run. The longer you play, the more certain it is that you will lose.

In casino games, patrons either do not understand what they are up against, or they understand but consider their losses a fair price to pay for an evening's entertainment.

Many unfortunate casino gamblers:

1. Don't understand that the game is biased against them.

2. Don't take their winnings and quit when they're ahead in the short run.

3. On losing, continue playing and redouble their efforts to pull even or win, ultimately (in the long run) compounding their losses.

A Little Restraint

While the casinos will not offer a fair game (like betting even money on the flip of a coin), they do understand that if they hammer you every time you come to play, sooner or later you will quit coming. Better to let you win every once in a while.

The Battle and the War

In casino gambling, the short run is like a battle, and either player or casino can win. However, the casino always wins the war. Players should stage commando raids: Get in, do some damage, and get out. Hanging around too long in the presence of superior force can be fatal.

Of course, it takes discipline to withdraw when you're winning, and it's even harder to call it quits when you're losing.

THE HOUSE ADVANTAGE

If casinos engaged in fair bets, they'd win about half the bets and lose about half. This arrangement would be more equitable, but it wouldn't pay the casino's mortgage or foot the bill for pirate battles, bargain room rates, or $2 steaks.

To ensure sufficient income to meet their obligations and show a profit, casinos establish rules and payoffs for each game to give the house an advantage. There are three basic ways the house establishes its advantage:

1. The rules of the game are tailored to the house's advantage
In blackjack, for instance, the dealer by rule always plays his hand
last. If any player busts (attains points exceeding 21), the dealer
wins by default without having to play out his hand.

2. The house pays off at less than the actual odds   Imagine a
carnival wheel with ten numbers. When the wheel is spun, each
number has an equal chance of coming up. If you bet a dollar on
number six, there is a one-in-ten chance you will win and a nine-
in-ten chance you will lose. (Gamblers express odds by compar-
ing the likelihood of losing to the likelihood of winning.) In this
case, nine chances to lose and one to win, or nine to one. If the
game paid off at the correct odds, you would get $9 every time
you won (plus the dollar you bet). Each time you lost, you would
lose a dollar.

But a casino can't play you even-up and still pay the bills. There-
fore, if a casino owner installed a wheel with ten numbers, he
would decrease the payoff. Instead of paying at the correct odds
(nine to one), he might pay at eight to one. If you won on your
last bet and were paid at eight to one, you would lose a dollar overall. Starting with $10, you lose your first nine bets (you're out $9)
and on your last, winning bet you receive $8 and get to keep the
dollar you bet. Having played ten times at the eight-to-one payoff,

House Advantages	
Baccarat	1.17% on bank bets, 1.36% on player bets
Blackjack	0.5% to 5.9% for most games
Craps	1.4% to almost 17%, depending on the bet
Keno	20% to 35%
Roulette	5.26% to 7.89%, depending on the bet
Slots	2% to 25% (average 4% to 14%)
Video poker	1% to 12% (average 4% to 8%)
Wheel of fortune	11% to 24%

you have $9 left, for a total loss of $1. The house's advantage in this game is 10% (one-tenth).

The house advantage for actual casino games ranges from less than 1% for certain betting situations in blackjack to in excess of 27% on keno and some slots. Although 1% doesn't sound like much of an advantage, it will get you if you play long enough. Plus, it adds up for the house.

Because of variations in rules, the house advantage for a game in one casino may be greater than the house advantage for the same game elsewhere. In most Las Vegas casinos, for instance, the house has a 5.26% advantage in roulette. At Sam's Town, however, because of the elimination of 00 (double zero) on certain roulette wheels, the house advantage is pared to about 2.7%.

Rule variations in blackjack swing the house advantage from almost zero in single-deck games to more than 6% in multiple-deck games with draconian rules.

The bottom line: Blackjack (played competently), baccarat, and certain bets in craps minimize the house advantage and give the player the best opportunity to win. Keno and wheel of fortune are sucker games. Slots, video poker, and roulette are not much better.

The money you take to the table is your "bankroll." When wagering money from your winning bets, you are adding to your original stake. In gambling parlance, this is "action," and it's very different from bankroll. When you risk your winnings in additional betting, you give the house a crack at a much larger amount than your original stake.

3. The house takes a commission   In all casino poker games and in certain betting situations in table games, the house will collect a commission on a player's winnings.

GAMES OF CHANCE AND THE LAW OF AVERAGES

Casinos offer games of chance (roulette, craps, keno, bingo, wheel of fortune, slots, baccarat) and games of chance *and* skill (poker and blackjack).

In games of chance, coins flip or wheels spin, and what happens is what happens. A player can guess the outcome but cannot influence it. Games of chance operate according to the law of averages. If you flip a coin ten times, the law of averages leads you to expect that half of the tosses will come up heads and the other half tails. If a roulette wheel has 38 slots, the law of averages suggests the ball will fall into a particular slot one time in 38 spins.

The coin, the roulette ball, and the dice, however, have no memory. They just keep doing their thing. If I toss a coin, it has no obligation to keep to the law of averages. The operative word, it turns out, is "averages," not "law."

What the law of averages *does* say is that, *in percentage terms,* the more times you toss the coin, the closer you will come to approximating the predicted average.

Games of Chance and Skill

Blackjack and poker are games of chance and skill, meaning that the knowledge, experience, and skill of the player can influence the outcome. All avid poker or bridge players can recall when they played for hours without being dealt a good hand. That's the chance part. In order to win (especially in blackjack, where there's no bluffing), you need good cards.

If you're dealt something to work with, you can use your skill to try to make your good hand even better. In casino poker, players compete against each other the same way they do at Uncle Bert's back home. The difference is that, in the casino, the house takes a small percentage of each winning pot as compensation for hosting the game (are you listening, Uncle Bert?). Although not every casino poker player is an expert, your chances of coming up against an expert are good. Our advice on casino poker: If you aren't a tough fish, don't swim with the sharks.

Blackjack likewise combines chance and skill. In blackjack, however, players compete against the house (the dealer). Players have choices and options in blackjack, but the dealer's play is bound by rules.

Still, in blackjack, as in every casino game, it's ludicrous to suggest that the house is going to surrender its advantage.

Playing It Smart

Experienced, noncompulsive, recreational gamblers play in a disciplined and structured manner. They recommend:

1. *Never gamble when you're tired, depressed, or sick.* Limit drinking. Alcohol impairs judgment and lowers inhibitions.

The Intelligence Test

If you have been paying attention, here is what you should understand:

1. All gambling games favor the house, and the house will always win in the long run.

2. It costs a lot to build, staff, and operate casinos, and casinos must attract many players in order to pay the bills and make a profit.

3. Casinos compete fiercely and offer incentives ranging from 50-cent hot dogs to free guest rooms to attract the right customers to their games.

Question: Given the above, what customer gets the best deal?

Answer: The person who takes advantage of all the incentives without gambling.

Question: What kind of customer gets the next best deal?

Answer: The customer who views gambling as recreation, gambles knowledgeably, bets sensibly, limits the amount he or she is prepared to wager, and enjoys all of the perks, but stays in control.

Question: What customer gets the worst deal?

Answer: The person who thinks he or she can win. This person will foot the bill for everyone else.

---

2. *Set a limit before you leave home on how much you're willing to lose gambling.* Do not exceed this limit.

3. *Decide which game(s) interests you, and know the rules before you play.* First-timers at craps or baccarat should take lessons (free at casinos). Virgin blackjack players should buy a good book and learn basic strategy. For all three,

observe games in progress for an hour or more before buying in. Shun games like keno and wheel of fortune, in which the house advantage is overwhelming.

4. *Decide how long you want to play, and devise a gambling itinerary consistent with your bankroll.* For example, you'll be in Las Vegas two days and want to play about five hours each day. If you have $500 to gamble, that's $250 a day. Dividing that by five hours, you come up with $50 an hour.

    Now, think of your gambling in terms of sessions instead of hours. You're going to play five sessions a day with $50 to wager at each.

5. *Observe a strategy for winning and losing.* On buying in, place your session allocation by your left hand. Play your session money only once during a session. Any time you win, return your original bet to the session-allocation stack (left hand), and place your winnings by your right hand. Never play chips or coins you have won. When you have gone through your allocation once, pick up your winnings (right hand) and quit. The difference between your original allocation and what you walk away with is your net win or loss for the session.

    During the session, bet consistently. If you're losing, don't up your bets in an effort to get even.

    If you doubled your allocated stake during a session (in this case, walked away with $100 or more), take everything in excess of $50 and put it aside as winnings, not to be touched for the remainder of your trip. If you won but didn't double your money, or if you had a net loss (less than $50 in your win stack), use this money in your next session.

6. *Take a break between sessions.*

7. *When you complete the number of sessions scheduled for the day, stop gambling.* Period.

GAMING INSTRUCTION AND RESOURCES

Most casino games are fairly simple, once you know what's going on. We recommend you join the free gaming lessons offered by

Where to Go for Lessons

Baccarat

Bally's
Caesars
  Palace
MGM Grand
Riviera

Blackjack

Bally's
Caesars
  Palace
Circus Circus
Excalibur
Harrah's
Lady Luck
Luxor
MGM Grand
Riviera
Sahara

Silverton
Stardust

Caribbean Stud

Harrah's
MGM Grand
Riviera
Stardust

Craps

Bally's
Caesars
  Palace
Circus Circus
Excalibur
Flamingo
Harrah's
Lady Luck
Luxor

MGM Grand
Riviera
Sahara
Sam's Town
Stardust

Let It Ride

Harrah's
MGM Grand
Riviera
Stardust

Pai Gow and Pai Gow Poker

Bally's
Caesars
  Palace
Harrah's

MGM Grand
Stardust

Poker

Monte Carlo

Roulette

Bally's
Caesars
  Palace
Circus Circus
Excalibur
Harrah's
Luxor
MGM Grand
Riviera
Stardust

Video Poker

Fiesta

casinos. Friendly and fun, the lessons introduce you to both the rules and the etiquette of games. You learn to play and bet without wagering money. Many casinos offer low-minimum-bet "live games" after the instruction. Gamblers' nonplaying companions also would benefit from the lessons. Spectating is more interesting if you know what's going on.

When "new games" are added, casinos generally offer instruction for a limited time. The latest rages are Red Dog poker and, owing to increasing Asian gamblers, Pai Gow and Pai Gow poker.

Written References and the Gambler's Book Club   If you can't find references on casino gambling at your local library or bookstores, call the Gambler's Book Club at (800) 634-6243 for a free catalog. The club's Las Vegas store is at 630 S. 11th St. (382-7555). It stocks single issues of the *Las Vegas Advisor*.

Funbooks, Matchplay, and Understanding the Marquees

Casino games are full of jargon. Most terms are clear from context, but those below are common in ads and coupons, and on marquees, and confuse many people.

Crapless Craps   Dice totals of 2, 3, 11, and 12 count as point numbers.

Double Exposure 21   A version of blackjack in which both of the dealer's cards are dealt face up.

Double Odds   The option in craps of making an odds bet twice the size of your line bet.

Funbooks   Booklets of coupons free from some casinos. Usually included are coupons for souvenir gifts, discount show tickets, discount meals, two-for-one or free drinks, and matchplay (see below). Some funbooks offer exceptional value; others are a hustle. On balance, coupon books are worth checking out.

Loose Slots   Slot machines that are programmed to pay off more frequently. The term is usually applied to machines with a return rate of 94% or higher, meaning that the house advantage is 6% or less.

Matchplay Coupons   Coupons from funbooks or print ads that can be redeemed for matchplay chips. These must be combined with an equal amount of your money on certain table game bets. If you win, you're paid for the entire bet in real money. If you lose, the dealer takes both your money and the matchplay chips.

Megabucks Slots   A statewide progressive slot machine network with grand jackpots in excess of $3 million.

Single-Deck Blackjack   Blackjack dealt from a single deck as opposed to two or more decks shuffled together.

Triple Odds   The option in craps of making an odds bet three times the size of your line bet.

WHERE TO PLAY

We receive a lot of mail from readers asking which casino has the loosest slots, the most favorable rules for blackjack, and the best odds on craps. We directed the questions to veteran gambler and tournament player Anthony Curtis, publisher of the *Las Vegas Advisor.* Here's his reply:

> *The best casino in Las Vegas to play blackjack, video poker, and other gambling games could be almost anyplace on a given day due to spot promotions and changing management philosophies. A few casinos, however, have established reliable track records in specific areas. Absent a special promotion or change in policy, I recommend these casinos as the best places to play each of the games listed:*

Blackjack
Slots A Fun

The only casino in Las Vegas dealing a single-deck game where the dealer stands on soft 17 and double down is allowed after splits. The combination results in a player advantage of .13% with perfect basic strategy.

Quarter Slots
Fitzgeralds

Competes hard for quarter slot players. Perhaps Las Vegas's best slot club.

Dollar Slots
Fiesta

Heavy-duty slot house. Good machine selection in the "Jackpot Blitz Zone." Periodic promo pays extra million dollars for hitting Megabucks there.

Craps
Binion's Horseshoe

Legendary dice house. Low minimums. Recently allowed up to 100x odds on $1 pass line bets.

Quarter Video Poker
Reserve

Best pay schedule available for every video poker variation on the floor. Several return more than 100%.

Dollar Video Poker
Reserve

More of the above. Also a good slot club with frequent multiple-point days.

Roulette Monte Carlo	Single zero in the heart of the Strip. The absence of the usual double zero lowers the casino's edge from 5.26% to 2.7%.
Baccarat Binion's Horseshoe	The mini-baccarat tables on the first floor charge a 4% commission on winning bank bets, compared to the standard 5%. This concession lowers the house edge from 1.06% to 0.6%.
Keno Silverton	A comparison of keno return percentages shows casinos that target locals offer the best chance of winning.
Bingo Showboat	Most elegant and airy bingo room in Las Vegas.
Poker Bellagio	Biggest room and most action around the clock.
Race and Sports Betting Caesars Palace	Big, bustling room covering all major events.
Let It Ride O'Shea's	Consistent $3 minimum.
Caribbean Stud Binion's Horseshoe	High reset on progressive with low minimums.
Pai Gow Poker Desert Inn	Best rules in town. Player may bank every other hand.

GAMBLING BUG'S MOST PAINFUL BITE

Some people can't handle gambling, just as some can't handle alcohol. The "high" described by the compulsive gambler parallels the experience of drug or alcohol abusers.

Compulsive gamblers attempt to use "the action" to cure for a variety of ills, much like some people use alcohol and drugs to lift them out of depression, anxiety, or boredom, and make them feel more "in control." The compulsive gambler blames circumstances and other people for the suffering he causes.

If this sounds like you or someone you love, get help. In Las Vegas, Gamblers Anonymous meets almost every night. Call 385-7732. Gamblers Anonymous also is in your local white pages.

SLOT MACHINES

Slot machines, including video poker, have eclipsed table games in popularity. Most casinos have allocated more than half of their floor space to slot machines. The popularity is easy to understand.

First, slots allow a person to gamble at at low or high stakes. Machines accept from a penny to $500 (special tokens). Quarter slots, however, are the most popular.

Second, many people like slots because no human interaction is required. A slot player can gamble and never be bothered by a soul.

Finally, slot machines appear to be simple. The only obvious thing you have to know is to put a coin in the slot and pull the handle. But there's more.

What You Need to Know before
You Play Slot Machines

Basics: All slot machines have a slot for inserting coins, a handle to pull or button to push to activate the machine, a visual display where you can see reels spin and stop on each play, and a coin tray that winnings may drop into.

Most slot machines have three reels, but some have as many as eight. Each reel has some number of "stops," positions where the reel can come to rest. Reels with 20, 25, or 32 stops are the most common. On each reel at each stop is a single symbol (cherry, plum, orange, etc.). If three of the same symbol line up on the pay line when the reel stops spinning, you win.

Many machines also pay for single cherries in the far left or far right position, two cherries side by side, or two bells or two oranges side by side with a bar on the end.

Almost all machines accept more than one coin per play (usually three to five). No matter how many coins the machine will take, only one is required to play.

If you put in additional coins (bet more), you buy:

1. Payoff schedules   Posted above the reel display are payoff schedules that show how much you can increase your payoff (if you win) by playing extra coins. Usually the increase is straightforward. If you play two coins, you win twice as much as if you play one coin; three coins, three times as much; and so on. Some machines, however, have a grand jackpot that pays only if the maximum number of coins has been played. If you line up the symbols for the grand jackpot but haven't played the maximum number of coins, you won't win. Always read and understand a machine's payoff schedule before you play. If it isn't clear, ask an attendant or find a simpler machine.

2. Multiple pay lines   When you play your first coin, you buy the pay line in the center of the display. By playing more coins, you buy additional pay lines. Each line you purchase gives you another way of winning. Make sure each line you buy is acknowledged by a light before you pull the handle.

Nonprogressive vs. Progressive Slot Machines   Nonprogressive slot machines have fixed payoffs. How much you would get for each winning combination is posted on the machines.

Progressive slot machines have a grand jackpot that grows until somebody hits it. After that jackpot is won, a new one starts to grow. Individual machines can offer modest progressive jackpots, but the really big jackpots (several thousand to several million dollars) are possible only on machines linked to other machines. Sometimes an "island," "carousel," or "bank" of machines in a casino is linked to create a progressive system. The more these machines are played, the faster the jackpot grows. The largest progressive jackpots, however, come from multicasino systems that may cover the state.

Progressives offer an opportunity to strike it rich, but they give fewer intermediate wins.

How Slot Machines Work

Almost all slot machines are controlled by microprocessors. This means machines can be programmed and are more like computers than mechanical devices. Each machine has a "random number generator" that we call a "black box." Each second, the black box spits out hundreds of numbers randomly selected from among about four billion available.

The numbers the black box selects trigger a set of symbols on the display, determining where the reels stop. Black boxes pump out numbers continuously, regardless of whether the machine is being played. If you are playing a machine, the black box will call up hundreds or thousands of numbers in the few seconds between plays while you sip your drink, put some money in the slot, and pull the handle.

There's no such thing as a machine that is "overdue to hit." Each spin of the reels is an independent event. The only way to hit a jackpot is to activate the machine at the exact moment the black box randomly selects a winning number.

Cherry, Cherry, Orange   The house advantage is known for every casino game except slots. With slots, the advantage is whatever the casino wants it to be. In Atlantic City, the maximum legal house advantage is 17%. There's no limit in Nevada. Interviews with ex–casino employees suggest, however, that the house advantage in Las Vegas ranges from about 2.5% to 25%, with most machines giving the house an edge of between 4% and 14%.

Casinos advertise their slots in terms of payout or return rate. If a casino says its slots return up to 97%, that means the house has a 3% advantage. We're skeptical when casinos advertise machines paying up to 98%. In most casinos, only a few slots will be programmed to return more than 92%.

Slot Quest   A slot machine that withholds only a small percentage of the money played is "loose," while a machine that keeps most of the coins it takes in is "tight." Because return rates vary among casinos and because machines in a casino are programmed to withhold differing percentages of coins played, slot players devote much energy to finding the casinos with the loosest machines. There are several theories on how to pinpoint these casinos.

Some say smaller casinos such as Slots-A-Fun and Silver City, which compete against large neighbors, must program their slots to provide a higher return to players. Alternatively, some folks play slots only in casinos patronized predominantly by locals (Gold Coast, Palace Station, Boulder Station, Fiesta, Texas Station, El Cortez, Gold Spike, Showboat, Sam's Town, Arizona Charlie's, Santa Fe). They reason that these casinos vie for regular customers and must offer competitive win rates. Downtown casinos competing with the Strip are likewise cast in the "we try harder" role.

Machines in supermarkets, restaurants, convenience stores, airports, and lounges are purported to be very tight.

Within a casino, veteran slot players theorize, the loosest slots are by the door or in the waiting area outside the showroom. Loose machines here, the theory goes, demonstrate to passersby and show patrons that the house has loose slots.

Of the theories for finding loose machines in a specific casino, the suggestion that makes the most sense is to select a casino and play there long enough to develop a relationship with the slot attendants. Be friendly. Engage them in pleasant conversation. If the casino has a slot club, join and use the club card so slot personnel will regard you as a regular. If the attendants are responsive and kind, and you win, tip them. After a couple of hours, the attendants will begin to take an interest in you. Ask them to point out a good (loose) machine. Tip them for the information and tip again if you do well on the machine. Don't blame them if you lose.

Maximizing Your Chances of Winning on the Slots   In any multiple-coin slot machine, you're more likely to win if you play the maximum number of coins. If you want to bet only 25 cents per play, you will probably be better off putting five nickels into a multiple-coin nickel slot than one quarter into a multiple-coin quarter slot. Never play a progressive machine unless you bet the maximum number of coins. To do otherwise is to contribute to a jackpot you have no chance of winning.

Common Sense

If you line up a winner and nothing happens, don't leave the machine. Jackpots sometimes exceed the coin capacity of the machine and must be paid by the cashier. Call an attendant. While you wait, don't play further on the machine. When the attendant arrives, check his casino employee identification.

If the pay lines fail to illuminate when you're playing multiple coins, don't leave or activate the machine (pull the handle). Call an attendant.

Slot Clubs and Frequent-Player Clubs

Most casinos have slot or frequent-player clubs. Their purpose is to foster customer loyalty by providing incentives. You can join a club in person at some casinos or apply by mail. No dues are charged. You receive a plastic membership card. This is inserted into certain quarter and dollar slots (including video poker machines). When your card is in the receptacle, you are credited for the action you give that machine.

Programs vary, but generally you are awarded "points" based on how long you play and how much you wager. Some clubs award points for both slot and table play. Accumulated points can be redeemed for awards ranging from casino logo apparel to discounts (or comps) on meals, shows, and rooms.

If you enjoy gambling all around town, you may never accrue enough points in one casino to earn a prize. Nonetheless, it's a good idea to sign up. Joining identifies you as a gambler on the casino's mailing list. You'll be offered discounts on rooms and other deals. Frequent business travelers should join their hotel's slot club.

VIDEO POKER

Never in casino gambling has a new game become so popular so quickly. All across Nevada, casinos are reallocating game-table and slot space to video poker machines.

In video poker, you aren't playing against anyone (no professional gamblers!). Rather, you're trying to make the best possible five-card-draw poker hand. On the most common machine, you insert your coin(s) and push a button marked "deal." Your original five cards are displayed on a screen. Below the screen and under each card pictured are "hold" buttons. After evaluating your hand and planning strategy, you designate the cards you want to keep by pressing the appropriate hold button(s). If you hit the wrong button or change your mind, most machines have an "error" or "erase" button, allowing you to revise your choices. When you press the hold button, the word "hold" will appear over or under that card on the display. Double-check the screen to make certain the cards you intend to hold are marked before you draw. If you don't want to draw any cards (you like your hand as dealt), press all five hold buttons.

When you're ready, press the button marked "draw" (on many machines, the same button as the deal button). Cards not held will be replaced. As in live draw poker, the five cards you have after the draw are your final hand. If the hand is a winner (a pair of jacks or better on most quarter or dollar machines), you will be credited the appropriate winnings on a meter. Retrieve these winnings by pressing the "cash-out" button and removing the coins from the tray. If you leave your winnings on the meter, you may use them to bet, eliminating the need to insert coins.

Winning hands and their respective payoffs are posted on or above the video display. As with other slots, you increase your payoffs and become eligible for jackpots by playing the maximum number of coins.

Both progressive and nonprogressive quarter and dollar video poker machines are available. Nonprogressives pay more on a full house (nine coins) and a flush (six coins) than progressives do (eight and five, respectively). Progressives feature a grand jackpot that builds until somebody hits it. Nonprogressives usually offer a bonus jackpot for a royal flush when the maximum coins are played.

Video poker machines are labeled according to these payoffs as "nine/six" or "eight/five" machines. Never play a progressive machine unless you're playing the maximum number of coins. By playing fewer than the maximum, you disqualify yourself for the grand jackpot. Plus, the return rate is lower than on a nonprogressives. The jackpot on a nonprogressive can sometimes exceed that of a progressive.

In addition to standard draw poker, games with jokers or deuces wild are also available. Jokers wild machines normally pay on a pair of kings or better, while deuces wild pays on three-of-a-kind and up. Casinos clean up on wild card machines because few players understand the strategy of play.

With flawless play, the house advantage on nine/six quarter and dollar machines ranges up from about 1/2% (0.5%), and for eight/five machines and wild card programs, from about 3%. On nickel machines, the advantage is about 5–10%.

TABLE GAMES

All casino games in which you interact with casino personnel or other players are called "table games." These include Blackjack, Craps, Wheel of Fortune, Roulette, Baccarat, Poker, Let It Ride, Caribbean Stud, Pai Gow Poker, and even Keno and Bingo: everything, in other words, except slots and other machines played by a single individual. The rules for all of these games vary from casino to casino. Some games (Wheel of Fortune, Craps, Baccarat) are purely games of chance, while others like blackjack and poker involve subtlety and skill. All table games are operated under the supervision of a casino employee, usually called a dealer (sometimes even when there's no dealing involved).

If you want to play one of the table games, we suggest availing yourself of the free lessons provided at most casinos. You will not only learn the rules, but also will be exposed to the protocol and the pace of play. Lessons almost always include a number of practice rounds where no real money is involved. Sometimes after the lesson students are invited to play for smaller than normal stakes.

Any game that appeals to you is all right if you're playing just for fun and pretty much expect to lose your money anyway. If, however, you want to give yourself a sporting chance of winning a little, you're well advised to limit your play to the games where the house has the smallest edge. These games are Blackjack, Baccarat, and pass line bets in Craps. Blackjack is a simple game, but has many variations, and requires some skill. Baccarat and the pass line bets in Craps do not require skill. Simply place your bet and the dealer will do the rest. Wheel of Fortune and Keno are sucker games and should be avoided. All the other games fall somewhere in-between.

Almost all table games require some minimum bet, so choose a table where the minimum is affordable. Also take a minute or so before buying in to observe the dealer. Is he or she personable and friendly? If the dealer has an attitude, so should you: find another table. Players at table games are routinely offered free drinks. This is part of the casino scene and does not obligate you in any way, except that it's considered good form to tip the waitress when your drink arrives.

For card games keep your hands above the table, and for all games, do not touch your bet once play in underway except as the rules of the game allow. Always feel absolutely free to quit whenever you want, or to switch tables.

Part Four

Shopping and Seeing the Sights

Shopping in Las Vegas

The most interesting shopping in Las Vegas is on the Strip at the Fashion Show Mall, The Forum Shops at Caesars Palace, and the Grand Canal Shoppes at the Venetian. Within walking distance of each other, they offer what may be the nation's most unusual concentration of upscale retailers. The Forum Shops and the Grand Canal Shoppes are not just retail areas; they're themed attractions. See them even if you don't like to shop. Fashion Show Mall's lure, by comparison, is its great lineup of big-name stores.

Anchoring Fashion Show Mall, at the intersection of Las Vegas Boulevard and Spring Mountain Road, are Saks Fifth Avenue, May Company, Neiman Marcus, Macy's, and Dillard's. Another 144 specialty shops include four art galleries and designer boutiques. This is the place to go for reasonable prices.

The Roman market–themed Forum Shops are connected to the Forum Casino in Caesars Palace. About 100 shops and restaurants line a re-created Roman street. Although the shops are indoors, simulated clouds, sky, and celestial bodies are projected on the vaulted ceilings to mirror the actual time outside. Statuary is magnificent; some are even animatronic. A new wing features an IMAX 3-D simulator attraction called *Race for Atlantis* (page 151). And The Forum Shops are expanding yet again.

The Grand Canal Shoppes mirror the modern-day canals of Venice. Ninety shops, boutiques, restaurants, and cafes are arrayed along a quarter-mile-long Venetian street flanking a canal on which gondolas navigate. A 70-foot ceiling simulates sky. The centerpiece is a replica of St. Mark's Square—without the pigeons.

Both the new Aladdin and Paris Las Vegas will include huge retail revues: a 450,000-square-foot shopping and entertainment complex in the case of the Aladdin and 31,000 square feet of upscale French boutique shopping in Paris's Rue de la Paix. Modest in size by Las Vegas shopping standards, the Rue de la Paix recreates a Paris street scene with cobblestone pavement and winding alleyways.

Most of the 190,000-square-foot Showcase complex, adjacent to the MGM Grand, is devoted to theme restaurants, a Sega electronic games arcade, a Coca-Cola museum, and an eight-theater movieplex.

The city's two large neighborhood malls are Boulevard Mall and the Meadows. Both have Sears, Dillard's, and Macy's. The 122-store Boulevard Mall on Maryland Avenue, between Desert Inn Road and Flamingo Road, also has Marshalls. The Meadows' 73 stores are on Valley View between West Charleston Boulevard and the Las Vegas Expressway (US 95).

About a mile south of Blue Diamond Road on Las Vegas Boulevard are 108 shops at the Las Vegas Factory Stores. North of Blue Diamond Road is a Belz Factory Outlet Mall with 109 stores. About an hour southwest on I-15 in Primm, Nevada, is Fashion Outlet Mall, offering themed dining and 100 outlet stores. Lists of shops at these locations are available in hotel brochure racks.

Unique Shopping Opportunities

Gambling Stuff   If you're in the market for a roulette wheel, blackjack table, or personalized chips, try the Gamblers General Store at 800 S. Main; call (702) 382-9903, or (800) 322-CHIP outside Nevada. Another option is Paulson Dice and Card, 2121 Industrial Road; call (702) 892-9096. For books and periodicals on gambling, we recommend Gamblers Book Club, near the intersection of South 11th Street and East Charleston; call (702) 382-7555.

Buy one-armed bandits at Vintage Slot Machines, 3379 Industrial Road, phone (702) 369-2323. The legality of possessing a slot machine (including video poker and blackjack) for personal use varies by state. Inquire at the store.

Head Rugs   The nation's largest wig and hairpiece retailer is Serge's Showgirl Wigs, 953 E. Sahara Ave. Serge's stocks more than

7,000 items and specializes in assisting chemotherapy patients. For a catalog, call (702) 732-1015.

Baseball Cards   Smokey's Sports Cards, possibly the nation's largest buyer, seller, and auctioneer of sports trading cards, is open every day at at 3734 Las Vegas Boulevard South, (702) 739-0003.

Zoot Suits   No kidding. For the coolest threads in town, try Valentino's Zootsuit Collection: Vintage Apparel & Collectibles at the corner of South 6th Street and Charleston. If you only want to zoot up for a special occasion, rentals are available. Call (702) 383-9555.

Seeing the Sights

When nongambling visitors look for something to do, they don't find Disney World, but they do find serious contenders for their time.

THE MGM GRAND ADVENTURES THEME PARK

The MGM Grand Adventures Theme Park is the nation's fourth movie-themed amusement park. But unlike Universal Studios Hollywood, Universal Studios Florida, and the Disney-MGM Studios at Walt Disney World, it doesn't include working production studios. It also falls far short of the high standard set by Disney.

Small by theme-park standards, it's about one-sixth the size of the Magic Kingdom at Walt Disney World. Six themed areas contain 10 rides and three theaters, plus restaurants and shops. The themed areas are so small that there's no sense of being in a self-contained environment. London Bridge is at the Salem Waterfront, a Dutch windmill edges Gold Rush Junction, and the Grand Canyon Rapids are in New Orleans.

This could be forgiven if attractions were top quality. Unfortunately, they aren't.

The only major attractions that live up to their press releases are Grand Canyon Rapids and the SkyScreamer. The rapids ride is wet and zippy and mostly maintains its theme's integrity. On SkyScreamer, you're trussed into a harness, hoisted up a 250-foot tower, and dropped. After 100 feet of free fall, you swing pendulum fashion to break the fall. It's truly thrilling—and it isn't included in the park's admission price.

MGM Grand Adventures Theme Park Ratings	
SkyScreamer	★★★★
Grand Canyon Rapids	★★★½
Chaos	★★★
Grand Carrousel	★★
Parisian Taxis	★★
Lightning Bolt	★★
Over the Edge	★★
Red Baron	★★
Les Bumper Boats	★★
Dueling Pirates	★★
Pedalin' Paddleboats	★½

The best of the park's three theater productions is Dueling Pirates, a movie stunt show.

Getting There The park is directly behind the MGM Grand Hotel at the intersection of the Strip and Tropicana Avenue. Pedestrians reach the park through either the hotel's lion entrance on the Strip or the auto entrance off Tropicana. Cars must drive west on Tropicana and use the auto entrance. Valet and self-parking are available. A monorail runs between Bally's and the MGM Grand. Also, buses and Strip trolleys serve the MGM Grand.

Admission Passing through the casino, guests follow the restaurant arcade to the complex's northeast corner, where Rainbow Bridge connects the hotel to the theme park. Ticket booths are on both sides of the bridge. Single-day admission, which includes all attractions, fluctuates wildly. At press time, prices were about $12 (including tax). Summer hours are 11 a.m.–7 p.m. As a rule, the park is open on weekends only in the spring and fall and is closed in winter except for certain holidays. Call (702) 891-1111 for more information.

OTHER MGM GRAND ATTRACTIONS

In 1999, the MGM Grand opened a 9,000 square foot lion habitatat that houses up to five of the big cats. The lions are on duty from 11 a.m. until 11 p.m. daily and admission is free. There is also, of course, an MGM Lion logo shop and the opportunity (for $20) to be photographed with a lion.

ADVENTUREDOME AT CIRCUS CIRCUS

Circus Circus's small but innovative amusement park, Adventuredome, is behind the main hotel and casino inside a climate-controlled glass dome atop the casino's parking structure.

The park resembles a western desert canyon, with artificial rock sculpted into caverns, pinnacles, and steep cliffs. A stream cascades 90 feet into a blue-green pool. Set among the rocks are a roller coaster, flume ride, and rides for young children. Embellishing the scene are life-sized animatronic dinosaurs, a re-created archaeological dig, and a replica of Indian cliff dwellings. A small theater features magic, and an arcade offers electronic games.

Adventuredome's top attractions are Canyon Blaster, the nation's only indoor, double-loop, corkscrew roller coaster, and Rim Runner, a three-and-one-half-minute water flume ride. Both wind among the rocks and cliffs.

The park's ticket plaza is on the mezzanine level, reached through the rear of the main casino. Plan to spend about $16–20 per person. All-inclusive passes and tickets to individual attractions are available. For current prices, call (702) 794-3939.

BELLAGIO ATTRACTIONS

The big draw at Bellagio is the Gallery of Fine Art Exhibition, displaying works by the world's master painters. Approximately 50 works are showcased in a new, larger gallery built in 1999. On entering you are issued an "audio wand" cassette player and earphones. By entering the number of a particular work on the audio wand, you can listen to a taped narrative describing the work and providing an anecdotal biography of the artist. Once admitted to the gallery, you can stay as long as you please. The exhibit is open daily from 9 a.m. until midnight. Tickets for both adults and children must be purchased on site at the gallery or at the ticket office near the sportsbook (less crowded). If you know when you're going to Las Vegas, you can make advance reservations by calling (888) 488-7111. (Bellagio guests can make reservations 90 days in advance; other visitors can book 7 days in advance.) If you have children in your party, be advised that they are allowed into the gallery from 9 a.m. until 11 a.m. only and must be accompanied by an adult.

Bellagio's free outdoor spectacle is a choreographed water fountain show presented every half-hour from 2 p.m. until midnight on the lake in front of the hotel. The five-minute production uses 1,200 fountains that blast streams of water as high as 200 feet. Almost 5,000 colored lights and musical accompaniment by Sinatra, Pavarotti, and Strauss, among others, complete the picture. It's pleasant and colorful but not necessarily something you should go out of your way to see.

LUXOR ATTRACTIONS

The Luxor offers two attractions inside the pyramid on the level above the casino. Designed by Douglas Trumbull, creator of the Back to the Future ride at Universal Studios, In Search of the Obelisk consists of a flight simulation. A seven-story IMAX theater operates round the clock; tickets are $7 ($8.50 for 3-D).

These attractions are much more sophisticated than anything at MGM Grand Adventures or Adventuredome.

LAS VEGAS HILTON ATTRACTIONS

Star Trek: The Experience is a 16-minute "experience" that culminates in a four-minute space-flight simulation. After exploring far reaches of the galaxy, trekkers are welcomed home at the gift shop.

Although the visuals are fuzzy, the experience offers twists and surprises and earns a first-place ranking among Las Vegas's simulator attractions. Hours are 10:30 a.m. to 11 p.m. daily. Go between 12:30 and 2 p.m. or after 4 p.m. weekdays. Admission of $14.95 includes tax. Hint: The entrance from "Deep Space Promenade" is free. For information, call (702) 732-5111 or (888) GO-BOLDLY.

STRATOSPHERE ATTRACTIONS

The 1,149-foot Stratosphere Tower offers unparalleled views of Las Vegas day and night.

A 12-level pod crowns the futuristic tower. The highest level is the boarding area for the High Roller roller coaster and Big Shot thrill ride. An outdoor observation deck is on Level 9; an indoor observation deck is on Level 8. Level 7 features a 220-seat lounge, and Level 6 houses an upscale revolving restaurant. Level 4 contains meeting rooms; Level 3, wedding chapels. Other levels are closed to the public.

The roller coaster is a snoozer. When working, it lumbers around the pod's perimeter. Visibility, the only thing this coaster has going for it, is limited by the tilt of the tracks, safety restraints, and other riders.

Big Shot, on the other hand, is cardiac arrest. Sixteen people at a time are blasted 45 miles per hour 160 feet straight up the needle atop the pod, then allowed to partially free fall. At the ascent's apex, it feels as if your seatbelt and restraint have evaporated, leaving you hovering 100 stories high. The ride lasts only a half-minute, but that's more than enough.

Elevators to the tower are at the end of the shopping arcade on the second floor. Tickets are sold in the elevator lobby and the casino. The queue by the elevators is usually shorter. Tower admission is about $6 for adults and $5 for children, seniors, active military, and Nevadans. Rides cost $6 each.

Expect an additional 20- to 40-minute wait for the rides on weekends. Even the line for the elevator down is long. However, if you walk to the restaurant, you can catch the down elevator with virtually no wait. If you must visit on a weekend, go as soon as the tower opens.

Another way to see the tower without a long wait is to dine at the Top of the World restaurant. Make reservations at least two weeks in advance. When you arrive in the elevator lobby, tell the greeter you have dinner reservations and show your confirmation number. You will be ushered into an express elevator. The restaurant is pricey, but the food is good and the view a knockout. Most patrons dress up. Buy Big Shot or High Roller tickets before ascending to the restaurant.

Tower hours are 10 a.m.–1 a.m. Sunday–Thursday and 10 a.m.–2 a.m. Friday and Saturday. For information, call (702) 380-7777.

Caesars Palace Attractions

So detailed is Caesars Magical Empire dining and entertainment complex that you could visit several times without exhausting its surprises (details on pages 47–48).

In 1998, Caesars launched *Race for Atlantis,* an IMAX 3-D, simulator experience at The Forum Shops. The IMAX visuals are well done, but the story line is muddled and not very compelling. The entrance is off the rotunda at the far west end of The Forum Shops. Go before or during a show at the rotunda's Fountain of the Gods. Queues are longest just after a fountain show.

Also at the Forum Shops is the 3-D Cinema Ride, a simulator attraction featuring a haunted graveyard, space flight, and submarine race. Other attractions at Caesars include the Omnimax Theater, off the casino, where documentaries are projected onto a six-story screen. IMAX admission is $7 for adults and $5 for children ages 2 to 12. Race for Atlantis costs $9.50 for adults and $6.75 for juniors (under 42 inches tall). Hours are 10 a.m. to 10 p.m. daily.

Mirage and Treasure Island Attractions

Mirage and Treasure Island attractions are top quality—and free. The two biggies are Treasure Island's pirate battle and the Mirage's erupting volcano. The pirate battle occurs, weather permitting, every 90 minutes from 4 to 10 p.m. (11:30 p.m. on Fridays and Saturdays in warmer months). As you face Treasure Island, the pirate ship is on your left and the British man-of-war enters from the right. The best vantage points are on the rope rail facing the man-of-war. On weekdays, claim your spot 15–20 minutes before show time; weekends, 35–45 minutes. You can see almost everything by joining the crowd at the last minute. If you're short or have children in your party, arrive early and stand by the rail.

The Mirage's volcano erupts every 15 minutes between 8 p.m. (6 p.m. in winter) and midnight, weather and winds permitting. Because shows are frequent, getting a rail-side vantage point isn't difficult. If you want to combine the volcano with a meal, grab a window table in the second-floor coffee shop of the Casino Royale across the street.

The Mirage displays some of Siegfried and Roy's white tigers inside its entrance (free). A nice dolphin exhibit is open from 11 a.m. to 5:30 p.m. weekdays and 10 a.m. to 5:30 p.m. weekends

($10; ages 10 and younger free). For information, call Mirage at (702) 791-7111 or Treasure Island at (702) 894-7111.

SAHARA ATTRACTIONS

The Speedworld simulator ride at the Sahara was inspired by Indy car racing. You can drive a racer in an interactive simulated race or strap in as a passenger for a 3-D movie race. Interactive racers respond exactly like real cars to braking, acceleration, and steering. You can even choose between manual or automatic (recommended) transmission. Your eight-minute race pits you against other drivers.

During the race, driving at high speed demands intense concentration. Visuals projected in front of your car are good but come at numbing speed. If you're motion-sensitive, the simulator will make your stomach spin.

Race once to understand how everything works. After that, it's more enjoyable, and you can be more competitive. Start on a simple course. After each race, you'll receive a computer-generated report on your performance. Each race you drive costs $8; the 3-D movie costs $3.

VENETIAN ATTRACTIONS

Like New York–New York down the Strip, it can be argued that the entire Venetian is an attraction, and there's a lot to gawk at even if you limit your inspection to the streetside Italian icons and the Grand Canal Shoppes. But there's more. The Venetian is host to the first Madame Tussaud's Wax Museum in the United States. Covering two floors and 28,000 square feet, the museum is about half the size of the original London exhibit. Approximately 100 wax figures are displayed in theme settings. Some, like Frank Sinatra and Tom Jones, were central to the development of the entertainment scene in Las Vegas.

A WORD ABOUT STRIP ROLLER COASTERS

Of the Strip's four roller coasters, the tight and smooth Canyon Blaster at Adventuredome offers the best ride, though it's shorter than the more visually appealing Manhattan Express at New York–New York. The Express's ride is jerky but provides a great view of the Strip. The Stratosphere's High Roller and the MGM Grand's "Exciting New Roller Coaster" are duds.

Free Stuff

The eye-popping Fremont Street Experience electric light show is produced on a four-block-long canopy over the Fremont Street pedestrian concourse downtown. Shows begin at dusk and run about once an hour through 11 p.m. on weekdays and midnight on weekends. Masquerade in the Sky, a musical Mardi Gras parade suspended from a track in the ceiling, circles the Rio's casino. The water and laser show at Sam's Town, starring animatronic animals and choreographed fountains, is staged four times daily. All three shows are free. Outdoor productions at Bellagio, Treasure Island, and the Mirage are also free of charge.

Other Area Attractions

If you have children, try **Scandia Family Fun Center** (phone (702) 364-0070) for miniature golf and the **Lied Discovery Museum** (phone (702) 382-5437) for an enjoyable afternoon of exploration and learning. Across from the Lied is the **Natural History Museum** (phone (702) 384-3466). **Wet 'n Wild** water theme park may be the best place in town for teens (phone (702) 737-3819). Look for **Wet 'n Wild** discount coupons in visitor guides.

The **auto collection at the Imperial Palace** (phone (702) 731-3311), showcasing more than 200 antique and historical vehicles, is worth the $6.95 admission, though discount coupons are available in visitor guides and the Imperial's casino.

The Liberace Museum (phone (702) 798-5595) on East Tropicana Avenue is hugely popular. Possibly the nation's most well presented celebrity museum, it's definitely more fun if you're a fan of the late pianist.

Showcase, adjacent to the MGM Grand, includes a giant Sega electronic games arcade, an eight-screen movie complex, and the World of Coca-Cola.

Natural Attractions near Las Vegas

The hour-and-a-half trip from the banks of Lake Mead to the high, ponderosa forests of Mount Charleston encompasses as much environmental change as driving from Mexico to Alaska.

Red Rock Canyon, the Valley of Fire, the Mojave Desert, and the Black Canyon of the Colorado River are world-class scenic attractions. In combination with the Spring Mountains' wet summits, they comprise one of the most dramatically diversified natural areas in North America.

Hoover Dam

Definitely worth seeing, Hoover Dam offers a film, guided tour, and theater presentation—all well done. Arrive by 9 a.m. Monday, Thursday, or Friday, and do the tour first. After 9:30, long lines form, especially Tuesdays, Wednesdays, Saturdays, and Sundays.

There's little advantage taking a bus tour to the dam. You still must wait in line for presentations.

Part Five

Dining and Restaurants

Dining in Las Vegas

The Las Vegas dining scene has undergone a revolution over the past five years. In an effort to attract customers in an increasingly competitive market, casino owners have convinced proprietors of many famous restaurants to open a branch in Las Vegas. Delmonico Steak House, Spago, Pinot, Morton's of Chicago, The Palm, Aureole, Le Cirque, Aqua, Chinois, and Star Canyon are a few examples. Celebrity chefs have been arriving with the regularity of Swiss trains and have opened scores of additional new restaurants. Upscale chains like Lawry's and Ruth's Chris are likewise well represented. Theme dining—so-called concept restaurants like House of Blues, Dive!, and Planet Hollywood—is also popular. And there's been a proliferation of brew pubs.

And today, if you want to avoid the expense-account joints or sense-assaulting themed eateries, Las Vegas offers some of the best local, independent restaurants found anywhere. Much improved in response to all the imported culinary talent, local restaurants offer ethnic diversity, exceptional food, and great value. They're easy to get to by cab or car, don't require reservations a month in advance, and offer ample parking.

Subsidized Dining and the Free-Market Economy

Las Vegas has two kinds of restaurants: those that are part of a hotel-casino and those that must make it on the merits of their food. Hotels' gourmet rooms pamper customers who are giving the house a lot of gambling action. Most patrons in hotel gourmet rooms are dining as guests of the casino. If you're a paying customer in the same restaurant, the astronomical prices you're charged subsidize the feeding of comped guests.

Restaurants independent of casinos work at a disadvantage. They don't have a captive audience of gamblers or convention-goers, they aren't subsidized by gaming, they aren't ideally located, and they compete with hotel buffets and casino gourmet rooms and meal deals.

Successful proprietary restaurants must offer something distinctive, as well as very good food at a competitive price.

All of this benefits the consumer. Folks of modest means can select among amazing steak, lobster, and prime rib deals offered by casinos or enjoy exceptional food at bargain prices at independent restaurants. People with little money gorge at loss-leader buffets.

So Many Restaurants, So Little Time

While there are hundreds of restaurants in Las Vegas, you will be able to sample only a handful during your stay. But which ones? Our objective is to point you to specific restaurants that meet your requirements for quality, price, location, and environment.

BUFFETS

Buffets, used by casinos to lure customers, are a Las Vegas institution. On average, there are around 40 to choose from. Most casinos operate their buffets at near cost or at a slight loss.

Most buffets serve breakfast, lunch, and dinner, changing their menus daily. Breakfast prices range from under $4 to $8. Lunch goes for $6–10; dinner, $7–19. The Rio Village Seafood Buffet is in a class of its own with lunch at $18.95 and dinner at $24.95 (and worth every penny).

Breakfast buffets differ little. If your hotel has one, it's probably not worth the effort to go elsewhere. At lunch and dinner, some buffets do a significantly better job.

If you crave well-seasoned meats and vegetables, ethnic variety, and culinary creativity, choose among our top eight buffets. If you prefer well-prepared simple foods, the remaining buffets in our hit parade do an excellent job with traditional American fare.

The Rio, Fiesta, Texas, and Sunset Stations, Main Street Station, Reserve, Harrah's, Resort at Summerlin, and Bellagio all have the new-style "superbuffets." The Rio started the craze in 1993

Buffet Speak	
Action Format	Food cooked to order in full view of the patrons
Gluttony	A Las Vegas buffet tradition that carries no moral stigma
Groaning Board	Synonym for a buffet; a table so full that it groans
Island	Individual serving area for a particular cuisine or specialty (salad island, dessert island, Mexican island, etc.)
Shovelizer	Diner who prefers quantity over quality
Fork Lift	A device used to remove shovelizers
Sneeze Guards	The glass/plastic barriers between you and the food

with its huge room, action cooking, and separate serving islands for a vast variety of ethnic choices. The Fiesta buffet is not as sprawling and various as the Rio's, but it has a higher level of quality, plus a monster rotisserie, specialty Cajun and Hawaiian selections, and Las Vegas's first and only coffee bar. Texas Station introduced a chili bar with nine selections and cooked-to-order fajitas. Bellagio is the most expensive superbuffet—and is worth every penny. The quality, quantity, and variety of food is unsurpassed in Vegas history. Main Street Station is the only superbuffet downtown, served in the most aesthetically pleasing buffet room in town. It's cuisine has a Hawaiian emphasis; the quality here is just short of Bellagio, and it's about half the price. The Reserve has wood-fired pizza, a Mongolian grill, and a daily seafood island. The Mirage Buffet is the Strip's version of the good Golden Nugget Buffet, with a few extras. Harrah's buffet gets an A for effort, a B for quality, and a C for value. Mandalay Bay's buffet is expensive and odd; it's small, congested, and slow. But Treasure Island, Palace and Boulder Stations, MGM Grand, Stratosphere, and Luxor are tried-and-true; you won't go wrong at any of these.

The most attractive settings are at Bellagio, the Resort at Summerlin, Main Street Station, the Flamingo, the Fremont, Caesars

Las Vegas's Ten Best Buffets		
Buffet	Quality Rating	Last Year's Ranking
1. Bellagio Buffet	98	not ranked
2. Upstair's Market Buffet at Resort at Summerlin	98	not ranked
3. Main Street Station Garden Court	95	5
4. Reserve Grand Safari Buffet	93	6
5. Fiesta Festival Buffet	92	2
6. Orleans French Market Buffet	91	not ranked
7. Bally's Big Kitchen Buffet	91	8
8. Texas Station Market Street Buffet	90	1
9. Rio Carnival World Buffet	89	3
10. Sunset Station—The Feast	82	4

Palace, Monte Carlo, Mirage, the Golden Nugget, Sunset Station, MGM Grand, and Treasure Island. Locals favor buffets at the Rio, Fiesta, and Texas, Palace, Sunset and Boulder Stations.

Several casinos have acceptable, though unexceptional, buffets. Alphabetically, they are:

Caesars Palace—Palatium Buffet

Circus Circus—Circus Buffet

Excalibur—New Round Table Buffet

Fitzgeralds—Molly's Coffee Shoppe and Buffet

Flamingo—Paradise Garden Buffet

Gold Coast Buffet

Harrah's—Fresh Market Square Buffet

Imperial Palace Emperor's & Imperial Buffets

Lady Luck Buffet

Las Vegas Hilton Buffet of Champions

Maxim—International Buffet

Mirage Buffet

Palace Station—The Gourmet Feast

Riviera World's Fare Buffet

Sahara Buffet

Sam's Town Great Buffet

San Remo Ristorante del Flori Buffet

Santa Fe Lone Mountain Buffet

Showboat Captain's Buffet
Stardust Warehouse Buffet
Treasure Island Buffet

Tropicana All-You-Can-Eat
Buffet

Seafood Buffets

Several casinos feature seafood buffets on Friday and sometimes other days. The best are the Rio's Village Seafood Buffet (daily), Fiesta's Hawaiian luau (Monday) and seafood night (Wednesday), and the Fremont's Seafood Fantasy (Sunday, Tuesday, and Friday).

The Rio's seafood buffet is the most expensive, yet quality and variety make it one of the city's great bargains. The Fiesta adds barbecued meats and poultry and Mongolian grill to its array of steamed, baked, stir-fried, broiled, and grilled seafood. The Fremont's spread isn't as extensive or expensive, but its quality and popularity are strong. The Gold Coast's seafood buffet Wednesday nights is popular with locals.

Buffet Line Strategy

Popular buffets develop long lines. To avoid crowds, go Sunday through Thursday and get in line before 6 p.m. or after 9 p.m. On weekends, arrive extra early or extra late. If a large convention is in town, choose among buffets that don't do a big convention business: Texas Station, Fiesta, Main Street Station, Palace Station, Boulder Station, Silverton, Showboat, the Fremont, and Reserve.

CHAMPAGNE BRUNCHES

Value-priced Sunday champagne brunches are plentiful, but more upscale, expensive champagne brunches with reserved tables, imported champagne, sushi, and seafood are having an impact. In general, the higher the buffet price, the better the champagne served. Bally's and MGM serve decent French champagne; California sparkling wine is the norm at the others. Reservations are accepted at these:

- **Sterling Brunch,** Bally's Steakhouse   739-4111
  This is by far the best brunch in town. At $49.95 per person (plus tax), it's also the most costly, but a good value if you're a big eater. The lavish selection of foods includes standard breakfast items, fresh sushi, real lobster salad, raw and cooked seafood, caviar, and French champagne. Pheasant and rack of lamb ap-

pear regularly. Desserts are awesome. Entrees change weekly. Available: 9:30 a.m.–2:30 p.m.

- **Grand Champagne Brunch at the Brown Derby,** MGM Grand   891-3110 (after 9 a.m.)
  A complete seafood bar, filet mignon, prime rib, and rack of lamb are regular features. Eggs Benedict and omelets are prepared to order. Adults, $28.95 per person includes tax (early bird price, 9–10 a.m., is $20); children 12 years and younger, $10.95; children younger than 5 years, free. Available: 9 a.m.–2 p.m.

- **The Steak House,** Circus Circus   734-0410
  Elaborate ice carvings and decorative food displays are a tribute to the chef's cruise-line background. Features many breakfast items, steak and seafood, entrees, and salads. Adults, $19.95 (all-inclusive); children 6–12 years, $9.95. Three seatings: 9:30 a.m., 11:30 a.m., and 1:30 p.m.

- **Champagne Brunch,** Ti Amo at Santa Fe   658-4900
  The best bargain brunch is in the indoor courtyard fronting the Santa Fe's restaurant row. A jazz trio serenades diners as they dig into pasta, pizza, omelets, carved filet mignon, smoked fish, clams, fresh fruit, and fine desserts, plus coffee liqueur and Bloody Marys. Adults, $12.95 plus tax and gratuity. Available 11 a.m.–5 p.m.

- **Garduno's Margarita Brunch,** Fiesta Hotel   658-4900
  There's no way Jose that even hearty eaters could down everything on this generous Mexican-style buffet. Colorful decor and margaritas galore make for happy dining. An omelet station, fajita station, peel and eat shrimp, crab legs, and fresh oysters as well as 15 or more Mexican specialties, including enchiladas, beef machaca, beef and chicken taquitas, chili and tacos. Salads and desserts, both Mexican and American. Come early or prepare to wait. Adults, $10.99 per person; children 4 to 8 years, $8.99. 10 a.m. to 3 p.m.

Other good brunches include those at Boulder and Sunset stations (menu also available), Caesars Palace (often features Bananas Foster), the Fiesta (substitutes margaritas for champagne), Desert Inn, Bellagio, and Golden Nugget.

MEAL DEALS

Many casinos have both buffets and dining deals. The latter includes New York strip, T-bone, and porterhouse steaks, prime rib, lobster, crab legs, shrimp cocktails, and breakfasts at giveaway prices.

While meal deals generally deliver what they promise, the extras of quality dining are missing. With few exceptions, specials are served in big, bustling restaurants.

It's often hard to take advantage of the specials. They're offered at odd hours, or the wait for a table is long. In our opinion, saving $5 on a meal isn't worth the hassle.

Our biggest complaint, however, is the lack of attention paid to the meal overall. It's difficult to get excited about a nice piece of meat that's served with droopy salads, stale bread, mealy potatoes, and canned vegetables.

Meal deals come and go. A book revised annually can't stay abreast. Your best resource for current deals is the *Las Vegas Advisor* monthly newsletter, (phone (800) 244-2224), or at Gamblers Book Club, 630 S. 11th St., (phone (702) 382-7555).

Steak   Our favorite special is the 16-ounce porterhouse steak dinner at the Redwood Bar & Grill in the California. Included are a relish plate, soup or salad, and steak accompanied by excellent potatoes and vegetables. Cost is $13 plus drinks, taxes, and tips. This special isn't on the menu; you must ask for it.

Binion's Horseshoe's legendary $2 late-night steak dinner bit the dust in 1997 but was revived at $3 in 1999. The California coffee shop has a late-night New York strip special for $3.99 (11p.m.–9 a.m.).

The Gold Coast coffee shop serves a great 16-ounce T-bone 24 hours a day for $7.95. A glass of draft beer is included.

Prime Rib   One of the best prime rib specials in a town full of prime rib specials is at the San Remo's Ristorante del Flori. A generous portion of meat with good sides is served 24 hours daily, and the restaurant is rarely crowded. Downtown, the Lady Luck coffee shop has good prime rib for $5.49 and $9.99, available 4–11 p.m. Up the block at the California, a smaller cut of meat during those hours costs $5.95.

For $4 or $5 more, dine in comparative luxury at Sir Galahad's in the Excalibur. The prime rib is excellent and accompanied by excellent sides, including Yorkshire pudding. Arrive by 6:30 p.m.

Other good specials, when available, are at Bally's ($9.95) and downtown at the Horseshoe. Jerry's Nuggett in North Las Vegas has deals for $7.95, $10.50, and $21 (the biggest piece of roast beef we've seen).

Lobster and Crab Legs   Lobster and steak (surf & turf) combos and crab leg deals appear regularly on casino marquees. Pasta Pirate at the California serves the best specials, but intermittently. When on, they feature a steak and lobster combo, a lobster dinner, or a king crab dinner, each $11–13 plus tax and tip. Wine is included.

Gold Coast's Mediterranean Room routinely offers an excellent crab special. Another good one is the $16 king crab special at El Cortez in Roberta's, Las Vegas's best bargain gourmet room.

The favorite among steak and lobster deals (which tend to be of lesser quality than steak, prime rib, and crab leg meal deals) is at Toucan Harry's at the Stardust ($9.95). Beware: Lobsters at buffets have the consistency of rubber.

Shrimp Cocktails   Casinos lure gamblers with inexpensive shrimp cocktails. Usually the shrimp are small and served in cocktail sauce in a tulip glass. The best and cheapest shrimp cocktails is at the Golden Gate downtown and at Joker's Wild in Henderson. Other contenders downtown are the Four Queens, Arizona Charlie's, and the Lady Luck.

Pasta and Pizza   Pasta Palace at Palace Station runs half-price specials on excellent pasta entrees, and Pasta Pirate at the California offers excellent designer pasta dishes. Find the best pizza at fast-food counters attached to Italian restaurants at Boulder Station and Sunset Station. Toscana's at the Rio serves a good slice of New York–style pizza.

Breakfast Specials   Our favorite is the huge ham and eggs special at the Gold Coast. Other worthwhile deals include steak and eggs at the Frontier, Arizona Charlie's, and the San Remo (24 hours), and the ham-and-eggs breakfast at the Horseshoe (4 a.m.–2 p.m.) and the Orleans breakfast buffet.

NEW RESTAURANTS

New entries in the burgeoning dining race include many we haven't profiled. Here's a taste:

Alex Stratta   Stratta's namesake restaurant at the Mirage pays homage to his many awards. It's pricey but excellent and is a culinary adventure led by the former chef of Mary Elaine's in Scottsdale. Dinner only.

Delmonico Steak House   Emeril Lagasse's gorgeous new steakhouse at the Venetian showcases an awesome wine selection, sophisticated interiors, and a gentlemen's bar with a smoking lounge. Steaks are prime.

First Floor Grill   This restaurant in the Four Seasons hotel at Mandalay Bay offers excellent steaks, seafood, and house specialties in a flower-filled dining room designed for relaxing. Exceptional wait staff.

Pinot Brasserie   A touch of France at the Venetian from Los Angeles's Joachim Spichal (Patina). Food is traditional brasserie fare with American touches.

Red Square   One side of the bar is solid ice to keep the vodkas at proper sipping temperature; the food is more eclectic than Russian, but it's reasonably priced and pretty good. Dinner only.

rumjungle   This restaurant and nightclub at Mandalay Bay is a wild, wonderful place for those who love a noisy, electric environment with their food. Food is cooked over an open firepit. Open until the wee hours.

Star Canyon   Stephan Pyles's Dallas favorite is now at the Venetian. Down-home, contemporary southwestern food in a cowboy-themed eatery.

Trattoria Del Lupo   Wolfgang Puck's new Italian at Mandalay Bay is another success. Pizzas, pastas, and a complete selection of rustic Italian dishes. Happy, colorful eatery with an expert young chef and an obliging staff.

The Restaurants
OUR FAVORITE LAS VEGAS RESTAURANTS

We profile what we consider the best restaurants in town. Each profile features headings that allow you to quickly check the restaurant's name, cuisine, Star Rating, cost, Quality Rating, and Value Rating.

Star Rating   The Star Rating is an overall rating of the entire dining experience, including style, service, and ambience plus taste, presentation, and quality of food. Only the best receive five stars, the highest rating. Four-star restaurants are exceptional, and three-star restaurants are above average. Two-star restaurants are good. One star denotes an average restaurant with capability in some area—for example, an otherwise forgettable place with great barbecued chicken.

Cost   The expense notation indicates the cost of complete meal: entree with vegetable or side dish, and choice of soup or salad. Appetizers, desserts, drinks, and tips are excluded.

Inexpensive	$14 and less per person
Moderate	$15–30 per person
Expensive	More than $30 per person

Quality Rating   On the far right of each heading are a number and letter. The number is a Quality Rating based on a scale of 0–100, with 100 being the highest (best) rating. The Quality Rating is based on taste, freshness of ingredients, preparation, presentation, and creativity of food. Price is no consideration. If you want the best food and cost is no issue, look no further than the Quality Rating.

Value Rating   If, however, you look for both quality and value, check the Value Rating, expressed in letters:

A	Exceptional value, a real bargain
B	Good value
C	Fair value, you get what you pay for
D	Somewhat overpriced
F	Significantly overpriced

Location   Just below the address is a zone name and number. The zone gives an idea of where the restaurant is. The zones we use are (maps on pages 6–11):

Zone 1	The Strip and Environs
Zone 2	Downtown
Zone 3	Southwest Las Vegas

Zone 4   North Las Vegas

Zone 5   Southeast Las Vegas and the Boulder Highway

If, for example, you're staying downtown and intend to walk to dinner, consider a restaurant in Zone 2.

Other Information   If you like what you see at first glance, read the rest of the profile for details.

OUR PICK OF THE BEST LAS VEGAS RESTAURANTS

Restaurants open and close all the time in Las Vegas. Our list is confined to establishments with a proven track record over a fairly long period. Newer restaurants (and older restaurants under new management) are listed but not profiled. Our list is highly selective. Excluding a restaurant doesn't mean it isn't good, only that it wasn't among the best in its genre. Some restaurants appear in more than one category.

The Best Las Vegas Restaurants

Name	Star Rating	Price Rating	Quality Rating	Value Rating
Adventures in Dining				
Emeril's (contemporary New Orleans)	★★★★½	Expensive	95	B
Bacchanal (Roman banquet)	★★★★	Expensive	94	B
Mamounia (Moroccan)	★★★½	Moderate	88	A
Marrakech (Moroccan)	★★★	Moderate	86	B
American				
Spago	★★★★★	Mod/Exp	94	C
Aureole	★★★★★	Expensive	98	C
Olives	★★★★	Mod/Exp	95	B
Kokomo's	★★★★	Expensive	93	C
Neros	★★★★	Expensive	90	C
Brown Derby	★★★★	Mod/Exp	87	C
Range Steakhouse	★★★½	Expensive	93	B
Diamond Lil's	★★★	Moderate	89	B
DIVE!	★★★½	Moderate	89	B
Hugo's Cellar	★★★½	Expensive	89	B

The Best Las Vegas Restaurants (continued)

Name	Star Rating	Price Rating	Quality Rating	Value Rating
Redwood Bar & Grill	★★★½	Moderate	89	A
Grape Street	★★★½	Inexp/Mod	87	A
Rainforest Cafe	★★★½	Moderate	86	B
Lawry's The Prime Rib	★★★½	Expensive	85	C
Magnolia Room	★★★½	Moderate	85	A
Top of the World	★★★½	Expensive	85	C
Wolfgang Puck Cafe	★★★½	Moderate	85	B
Caribbean Cabana	★★★	Moderate	80	A
Kathy's Southern Cooking	★★★	Inexpensive	80	A
Philips Supper House	★★★	Moderate	80	A
Asian				
China Grill	★★★★	Mod/Exp	89	B
China Grill Cafe & Zen Sum	★★★½	Inexp/Mod	85	B
Barbecue				
Sam Woo Bar-B-Q	★★★	Inexpensive	89	A
Brazilian				
Samba Grill	★★★★	Moderate	90	A
Brewpub				
Barley's	★★★	Inexpensive	86	A
Triple Seven Brewpub†	★★★	Inexp/Mod	85	A
California-Continental				
Drai's	★★★★½	Mod/Exp	96	B
Chinese (see also Dim Sum)				
Chin's	★★★★	Expensive	94	C
Fortune	★★★★	Mod/Exp	93	C
Chang	★★★½	Moderate	88	B
Peking Market	★★★½	Moderate	87	B
Chungking East	★★★½	Inexpensive	85	A
Sam Woo Bar-B-Q	★★★	Inexpensive	89	A
Cathay House	★★½	Moderate	80	C
Noodles	★★★½	Moderate	93	B

† No profile

The Best Las Vegas Restaurants (continued)

Name	Star Rating	Price Rating	Quality Rating	Value- Rating
Chinese/French				
Mayflower Cuisinier	★★★★½	Mod/Exp	94	B
Chinois	★★★★	Mod/Exp	96	A
Continental/French				
Bistro Le Montrachet	★★★★★	Mod/Exp	98	C
Palace Court	★★★★★	Expensive	98	C
Picasso	★★★★★	Expensive	98	C
Napa	★★★★★	Expensive	95	C
Monte Carlo	★★★★½	Expensive	95	C
Andre's	★★★★½	Expensive	90	C
Buccaneer Bay Club	★★★★	Moderate	96	B
Fiore	★★★★	Mod/Exp	95	B
Michael's	★★★★	Very Exp	93	D
Gatsby's	★★★★	Expensive	90	C
Seasons	★★★★	Expensive	90	D
Isis	★★★½	Expensive	90	B
Swiss Cafe	★★★½	Moderate	89	B
Café Nicolle	★★★½	Moderate	88	B
Pamplemousse	★★★½	Expensive	87	D
Burgundy Room	★★★½	Mod/Exp	85	B
Creole/Cajun				
VooDoo Cafe and Lounge	★★★½	Mod/Exp	85	C
Dim Sum (see also Chinese)				
Chang	★★★½	Moderate	88	B
Mirage Noodle Kitchen†	★★★	Moderate	85	B
Cathay House	★★½	Moderate	80	C
Eclectic				
Cheesecake Factory	★★★½	Moderate	89	A
Greek				
Magnolia Room	★★★½	Moderate	85	A
Tony's Greco Roman†	★★★	Moderate	81	B

† No profile

The Best Las Vegas Restaurants (continued)

Name	Star Rating	Price Rating	Quality Rating	Value Rating
Indian				
Shalimar	★★★½	Mod/Exp	86	C
Italian				
Terrazza	★★★★½	Expensive	95	C
Piero's	★★★★½	Expensive	92	C
Stefano's	★★★★	Expensive	94	C
Antonio's	★★★★	Mod/Exp	90	B
Tre Visi/La Scala	★★★½	Mod/Exp	94	B
Manhattan	★★★½	Mod/Exp	92	B
Mortoni's	★★★½	Mod/Exp	90	B
Ristorante Italiano	★★★½	Expensive	91	C
Anna Bella	★★★½	Inexp/Mod	89	A
Bootlegger	★★★½	Moderate	89	A
Ferraro's	★★★½	Mod/Exp	89	C
North Beach Cafe	★★★½	Moderate	89	A
Bertolini's	★★★½	Moderate	88	B
Fellini's	★★★½	Mod/Exp	87	A
Venetian	★★★½	Mod/Exp	87	B
Alta Villa	★★★½	Moderate	85	A
Bocacio Organico	★★★½	Moderate	86	B
Circo (Osteria Del)	★★★½	Mod/Exp	86	B
Magnolia Room	★★★½	Moderate	85	A
Il Fornaio	★★★	Mod/Exp	87	B
Sfuzzi	★★★	Moderate	82	B
Japanese (see also Sushi)				
Tokyo	★★★½	Moderate	85	B
Noodles	★★★½	Moderate	93	B+
Fuji	★★★	Inexp/Mod	84	B
Lobster				
Alan Alberts	★★★½	Expensive	89	C
Rosewood Grille	★★★½	Expensive	88	C
Lobster House†	★★★½	Expensive	89	C+

The Best Las Vegas Restaurants (continued)

Name	Star Rating	Price Rating	Quality Rating	Value Rating
Mediterranean				
Olives	★★★★	Mod/Exp	95	B
Mexican/Southwestern				
Coyote Cafe	★★★★	Mod/Exp	90	B
Garduno's Chili Packing Co.	★★★½	Inexp/Mod	89	B
Viva Mercado's	★★★½	Moderate	86	A
Ricardo's	★★★½	Moderate	85	B
Lindo Michoacan	★★★	Moderate	84	A
Middle Eastern				
Habib's	★★★½	Moderate	88	C
Jerusalem (Kosher)	★★½	Inexp/Mod	80	B
Moroccan				
Mamounia	★★★½	Moderate	88	A
Marrakech	★★★	Moderate	86	B
Persian				
Habib's	★★★½	Moderate	88	C
Prime Rib				
Sir Galahad's	★★★½	Moderate	89	A
Redwood Bar & Grill	★★★½	Moderate	87	A
Lawry's The Prime Rib	★★★½	Expensive	85	C
Philips Supper House	★★★	Moderate	80	A
Seafood				
Aqua	★★★★★	Expensive	98	C
Buzios	★★★★	Mod/Exp	93	A
Kokomo's	★★★★	Expensive	93	C
The Tillerman	★★★½	Mod/Exp	87	C
Pasta Pirate	★★★½	Moderate	86	A
The Broiler	★★★	Moderate	85	A
Steak				
Ruth's Chris Steak House	★★★★	Expensive	94	C
Kokomo's	★★★★	Expensive	93	C

The Best Las Vegas Restaurants (continued)

Name	Star Rating	Price Rating	Quality Rating	Value Rating
Prime	★★★★	Expensive	93	C
The Palm	★★★★	Expensive	90	C
Samba Grill	★★★★	Moderate	90	A
Alan Alberts	★★★½	Expensive	89	C
Morton's	★★★½	Expensive	89	C
Rosewood Grille	★★★½	Expensive	88	C
Redwood Bar & Grill	★★★½	Moderate	87	A
The Steak House	★★★½	Moderate	86	B
Billy Bob's Steakhouse	★★★	Mod/Exp	88	B
Yolie's	★★★	Moderate	86	B
The Broiler	★★★	Moderate	85	A
Binion's Ranch Steakhouse	★★★	Moderate	82	B
Sushi (see also Japanese)				
Chinois	★★★★	Mod/Exp	96	A
Teru Sushi	★★★½	Mod/Exp	89	C
Tokyo	★★★½	Moderate	85	B
Hamada of Japan †	★★★	Mod/Exp	84	C
San Remo Sushi Bar†	★★★	Expensive	84	C
Thai				
Noodles	★★★½	Moderate	93	B
Lotus of Siam	★★★	Moderate	85	A
Vietnamese				
Saigon	★★★	Inexp/Mod	83	A
Noodles	★★★½	Moderate	93	B+
Rooms with a View				
Top of the World (American)	★★★½	Expensive	85	C
VooDoo Cafe and Lounge	★★★½	Mod/Exp	85	C
Cathay House (Chinese)	★★½	Moderate	80	C

† No profile

More Recommendations

The Best Bagels

Bagel Oasis 9134 W. Sahara Ave., 363-0811
The best bagels in town, New York–style; baked daily; large selection.

Harrie's Bagelmania 855 E. Twain Ave. (at Swenson),
  369-3322
Baked on the premises; garlic and onion among the choices.

The Best Bakeries

Albina's Italian Bakery 3035 E. Tropicana Ave. (in the Wal-
  Mart Center), 433-5400
Classic Italian pastries; baba au rhum, with and without custard;
cheesecakes; variety of cookies.

Great Buns 3270 E. Tropicana Ave. (at Pecos), 898-0311
Commercial and retail. Fragrant rosemary bread, sticky buns, and
apple loaf are good choices. New items added regularly.

Rancho Bakery 3675 S. Rainbow Blvd. #107–163,
  870-6449
Ethnic specialties and party cakes; variety of breads and fancy
cookies.

The Best Brew Pubs

Barley's Casino and Brewing Company 4500 E. Sunset
  Road, Suite 30, Henderson, 458-2739
Reminiscent of old Las Vegas, Barley's features a small casino, at-
tractive decor, and comfort foods galore.

Gordon Biersch Brewpub 3987 Paradise Road (Hughes
  Center), 312-5247
Upbeat brewery restaurant with contemporary menu; surpris-
ingly good food, reasonably priced.

Holy Cow! 2423 Las Vegas Boulevard, South, 732-2697
Tri-level, barn-styled bar with comical cow decor; 24-hour food
service.

Monte Carlo Pub & Brewery Monte Carlo, 730-7777
Faux warehouse setting. Six beers brewed on the premises, 18 pizzas, plus sandwiches and pastas.

Triple Seven Brewpub   200 N. Main St. (Main Street
  Station), 387-1896
Late-night happy hour with bargain brews and food specials. Open
24 hours.

The Best Burgers

Kilroy's   1021 S. Buffalo Drive (at West Charleston), 363-4933
Half-pound burgers, choice of 15 toppings.

Lone Star   1290 E. Flamingo Road, 893-0348; 1611 S.
  Decatur Blvd., 259-0105
Cheese, Bubba, Texas, Mexi, or Willie half-pounders on toasted
onion bun.

Champagne Cafe   3557 S. Maryland Parkway, 737-1699
Classic half-pounder with creative toppings.

Sneakers   2250 E. Tropicana Ave. (at Eastern), 798-0272
Hefty burgers plus sports on TV.

Tommy's Hamburgers   2635 E. Tropicana Ave., 458-2533
Eat in or carry out.

The Best Delis

Freddy "G's" Deli and Diner   325 Hughes Center,
  892-9955
Full service New York–style deli; breakfast, lunch, and dinner.

Samuel's Deli   2744 N. Green Valley Parkway, Henderson,
  454-0565
Deli, bakery, and restaurant. Home cooking and giant matzo balls.

Siena Deli   2250 E. Tropicana Ave. (at Eastern), 736-8424
Everything Italian and homemade. Excellent bread baked every
morning. Local favorite for Italian grocery items.

Stage Deli   The Forum Shops at Caesars, 893-4045
Las Vegas branch of New York's famous pastrami palace; enormous menu of Jewish specialties, including triple-decker sandwiches and 26 desserts.

The Best Espresso and Dessert

Café Nicolle   4760 W. Sahara Ave. (at Decatur), 870-7675
Sidewalk café west; cooling mist in summer.

Coffee Pub   2800 W. Sahara Ave., 367-1913
Great breakfast and lunch location, imaginative menu.

Java Centrale   2291 N. Green Valley Parkway, 434-3112
Soups, sandwiches, chocolate-raspberry-bash pie, English scones.

Jitters Gourmet Coffee   2457 E. Tropicana Ave. (at Eastern), 898-0056; 8441 W. Lake Mead Blvd. (Summerlin location), 256-1902
Many coffee varieties; homemade muffins; sandwiches, brownies, truffles. Local hangout.

La Piazza   Caesars Palace, 731-7110
Pies, cakes, and cookies to eat in or take out.

Spago   The Forum Shops at Caesars, 369-6300
Wolfgang Puck's pastry chef creates imaginative delicacies.

Starbucks Coffee Houses   Many area locations.

The Best Oyster & Clam Bars
Buzios   Rio, 252-7697
Oyster stews, cioppino, shellfish, and pan roasts. Table service or oyster bar.

The Best Pizza
Bootlegger   5025 S. Eastern Ave. (at Tropicana), 736-4939 or 736-8661 (laugh line)
Great selection; crisp, tender, homemade crust.

California Pizza Kitchen   Mirage, 791-7111; Golden Nugget, 385-7111
Trendy. Low-cal versions without cheese available. No takeout.

Metro Pizza   4001 S. Decatur Blvd. (at Flamingo), 362-7896; 3870 E. Flamingo Road (at Sandhill), 458-4769; 2250 E. Tropicana Ave. (at Eastern), 736-1955
Fast service, generous cheese. Try the Old New York with thick-sliced mozzarella and plum tomatoes.

Spago   The Forum Shops at Caesars, 369-6300
Wolfgang Puck's regular specials include spicy shrimp, duck sausage, and smoked salmon with dill cream and caviar.

Venetian   3713 W. Sahara Ave., 876-4190
Las Vegas favorite; pizza with greens and olive oil (no cheese) is popular.

The Best Soup and Salad Bars

Paradise Garden Cafe   Flamingo Hilton, 733-3111
Magnificent display at lunch; large choice of seafood added at dinner.

Souper Salad   2051 N. Rainbow, 631-2604; 4022 S. Maryland Parkway, 792-8555; 4712 W. Sahara Ave., 870-1444
Moderate prices, many combinations shiny, clean, inexpensive.

Restaurants with a View

VooDoo   Rio Hotel and Casino, 252-7777
Atop the Rio tower. Offers complete view of the city, Cajun/Creole cooking, and late-night lounge.

ALAN ALBERTS	★★★½
Steak/Lobster	Expensive

Epicenter Plaza, North of the MGM Grand; 740-4421
Strip Zone 1

Dinner: Daily, 5–11:30 p.m.
Comments: Classic steakhouse. Generous portions. Lobsters priced fairly. Combination of appetizers a meal in themselves.

ALTA VILLA	★★★½
Italian	Moderate

Flamingo Hilton; 733-3111
Strip Zone 1

Dinner: Friday–Tuesday, 5:30–11 p.m.; Wednesday and Thursday, closed.
Comments: Vine-covered piazza. Strolling guitarist.

ANDRE'S   ★★★★½

Continental/French   **Expensive**

401 S. 6th St.; 385-5016
Downtown Zone 2

Monte Carlo Hotel; 798-7151
Strip Zone 1

Dinner: Daily, 6–9:30 p.m.
Comments: Country French; in historic area. Spectacular wine-maker dinners; get on mailing list. Vintages to 1830 in wine cellar. Downtown location closed in July.

ANNA BELLA   ★★★½

Italian   **Inexpensive/Moderate**

3310 Sandhill Rd. at Desert Inn; 434-2537
Southeast Zone 5

Dinner: Tuesday–Sunday, 4:30–10 p.m.; Monday, closed.
Comments: Charming neighborhood restaurant. Delicious food. A real find.

ANTONIO'S   ★★★★

Italian   **Moderate/Expensive**

Rio, 3700 W. Flamingo Rd.; 252-7777
Strip Zone 1

Dinner: Daily, 5–11 p.m.
Comments: Local favorite. Domed ceiling replicates sky. Complimentary after-dinner liqueur.

AQUA   ★★★★★

Contemporary seafood   Expensive

Bellagio; 693-7223
Strip Zone 1

Dinner: Every night, 5:30–11 p.m.
Comments: Elegant yet relaxed decor. This San Francisco transplant wins raves for service, food, and decor. Reservations are difficult to obtain.

AUREOLE   ★★★★★

American   Expensive

Mandalay Bay; 632-7401
Strip Zone 1

Dinner: Every night, 5–11 p.m.; lounge open 5 p.m–midnight.
Comments: A four-story wine tower dominates the entrance to this exceptional restaurant. Try the superb tasting menu (for the entire table). À la carte menu.

BACCHANAL   ★★★★

Roman banquet   Expensive

Caesars Palace; 731-7731
Strip Zone 1

Dinner: Tuesday–Saturday, seatings at 6–6:30 p.m. and 9–9:30 p.m.; Sunday and Monday, closed.
Comments: Roman garden with fountains and special effects. More for fun, but the food is surprisingly good.

BARLEY'S ★★★

Brewpub	Inexpensive

Town Center, 4500 E. Sunset, Green Valley; 458-2739
Southeast Zone 5

Open: Brewer's Cafe: Sunday–Thursday, 11 a.m.–10 p.m.; Friday and Saturday, 7 a.m.–11 p.m.
Pizza Parlor: Sunday–Thursday, 11 a.m.–10 p.m.; Friday and Saturday, 7a.m.–11 p.m.
Bar menu: 24 hours, breakfast 11 p.m.–7 a.m.
Comments: Comfort foods galore. Gleaming brewery. Small casino. Interactive fountain is wonderful entertainment.

BERTOLINI'S ★★★½

Italian	Moderate

The Forum Shops at Caesars; 735-4663
Strip Zone 1

Lunch & dinner: Sunday–Thursday, 11 a.m.–midnight; Friday and Saturday, 11 a.m.–1 a.m.
Comments: Beautiful interior. Sidewalk cafe overlooks Forum's noisy but photogenic Roman fountain.

BILLY BOB'S STEAKHOUSE & SALOON ★★★

Steak	Moderate/Expensive

Sam's Town, Boulder Highway; 456-7777
Southeast Zone 5

Dinner: Daily, 4:30–10 p.m.
Comments: Western-themed eatery with mighty fine grub. Robotic critters in lovely park. Laser show after dusk.

BINION'S RANCH STEAKHOUSE   ★★★

Steak   Moderate

Binion's Horseshoe Hotel; 382-1600
Downtown Zone 2

Dinner: Daily, 6–10:30 p.m.
Comments: Western decor, friendly service, large portions.
Panoramic view.

BISTRO LE MONTRACHET   ★★★★★

Contemporary French   Moderate/Expensive

Las Vegas Hilton; 732-5111
Strip Zone 1

Lunch: Friday and Saturday, 12–2 p.m.
Dinner: Bistro, 6–9:30 p.m.; dining room, 6–9:30 p.m. (closes
occasionally in low season; call ahead).
Comments: Contemporary bistro, elegant dining. Each dish a
work of art.

BOCACIO ORGANICO   ★★★½

Organic Italian   Moderate

Desert Inn Road; 699-9980
Southeast Zone 5

Lunch: Monday–Friday, 11:30 a.m.–2:30 p.m.
Dinner: Every night, 5–11 p.m.
Comments: Small but pleasant. The only organic Italian in town.
All ingredients are certified organic.

BOOTLEGGER ★★★½

Italian   Moderate

5025 S. Eastern Ave. (at Tropicana); 736-4939 or 736-8661 (laugh line)
Southeast Zone 5

Lunch & dinner: Tuesday–Friday, 11 a.m.–11 p.m.; Saturday
and Sunday, 4 p.m–11 p.m; Monday, closed.
Comments: Turn-of-the-century Italian decor. Reduced-fat dishes
of Project Lean, plus vegetarian. Very good seafood. Family-run.

THE BROILER ★★★

Steak/Seafood   Moderate

Boulder Station, Boulder Hwy. and Desert Inn Rd.; 432-7777
Southeast Zone 5

Brunch: Sunday, 10 a.m.–3 p.m.
Dinner: Sunday–Thursday, 5–10 p.m.; Friday and Saturday,
5–11 p.m.
Comments: Desert decor. Low-cholesterol fish selections.
Brunch a fine value.

BROWN DERBY ★★★★

American   Moderate/Expensive

MGM Grand; 891-7300
Strip Zone 1

Dinner: Daily, 5:30–11:00 p.m.
Comments: Re-creation of Hollywood's Brown Derby, with nos-
talgic items and original recipes.

BUCCANEER BAY CLUB   ★★★★½

Continental   Moderate

Treasure Island; 894-7111
Strip Zone 1

Dinner: Every day, 5–10:30 p.m.
Comments: Request table overlooking Buccaneer Bay, scene of
sea battles in front of Treasure Island.

BURGUNDY ROOM   ★★★½

Continental   Moderate/Expensive

Lady Luck Hotel; 477-3000
Downtown Zone 2

Dinner: Daily, 5–11 p.m.
Comments: Plush and intimate. Good selection of entrees.

BUZIOS   ★★★★

Seafood   Moderate/Expensive

Rio; 252-7697
Strip Zone 1

Lunch & dinner: Daily, 11 a.m.–11 p.m.
Comments: Alabaster chandeliers hang from canvas-tented ceiling. Irresistible breads. Counter service available.

CAFÉ NICOLLE ★★★½

Continental   Moderate

4760 W. Sahara Ave.; 870-7675
Southwest Zone 3

Lunch & dinner: Monday–Saturday, 11 a.m.–10:30 p.m.; Sunday, closed.
Comments: Restaurant and European-style outdoor cafe. Lounge entertainment nightly except Sunday.

CARIBBEAN CABANA ★★★

Island/American   Moderate

3190 West Sahara; 873-3345
Zone 3

Lunch & dinner: 24 hours
Comments: Large restaurant with Caribbean colors and accessories. A favorite hangout. Those expecting spicy island flavors will be disappointed. Ask your server to kick up the spice or add it at the table. 24-hour eatery.

CATHAY HOUSE ★★½

Cantonese/Dim Sum   Moderate

5300 Spring Mountain Rd.; 876-3838
Southwest Zone 3

Lunch: Daily, 11 a.m.–2:30 p.m.
Dinner: Daily, 3–10:30 p.m.
Comments: Picture windows overlook Strip. Good selection of dim sum from carts. Asians get better service.

CHANG   ★★★½

Chinese/Dim Sum   Moderate

Gold Key Shopping Center, Strip and
Convention Center Dr.; 731-3388
Strip Zone 1

Bally's; 739-4111
Strip Zone 1

Gold Key: Lunch and Dinner: daily, 10 a.m.–midnight; dim
sum: daily, 10 a.m.–3 p.m.
Bally's: Lunch: daily, 11:30 a.m.–2:30 p.m.; dinner: daily, 6–11
p.m.; no dim sum at this location.
Comments: Chinese art and artifacts. Excellent assortment of
dim sum.

CHEESECAKE FACTORY   ★★★½

Eclectic   Moderate

The Forum Shops at Caesars Palace; 792-6888
Strip Zone 1

Lunch & dinner: Monday–Thursday, 11:10 a.m. (after the first
Atlantis show) to 11:30 p.m.; Friday and Saturday, 11:10
a.m.–12:30 a.m; Sunday, 10a.m.–11:30 p.m.
Brunch: Sunday, 10 a.m.–2 p.m.
Comments: People-watch on patio. Egyptian-themed dining
room. Share a dish rather than forgo cheesecake.

CHINA GRILL   ★★★★

Asian inspired   Moderate/Expensive

Mandalay Bay; 450-5522
Strip Zone 1

Dinner: Sunday–Thursday, 5:30–11 p.m.; Friday and Saturday,
5:30 p.m.–midnight.
Comments: Highly original furnishings and lighting and contemporary art. Comfy lounge. Food portions are sized to be shared.

CHINA GRILL CAFE & ZEN SUM   ★★★½

Asian eclectic   Inexpensive/Moderate

Mandalay Bay; 632-8324
Strip Zone 1

Lunch & dinner: Every day, 11:30 a.m.–midnight.
Bar: Sunday–Wednesday, 11 a.m.–1 a.m.; Thursday–Saturday,
11 a.m.–2 a.m.
Comments: Conveyor-belt dim sum bar. The design includes
video and robotic features—it's pure funk. Kids love this eatery.

CHINOIS   ★★★★

French-Chinese   Moderate/Expensive

The Forum Shops at Caesars Palace; 737-9700
Strip Zone 1

Lunch & dinner: Daily, 11:30 a.m.–10:30 p.m.
Comments: Enchanting Asian decor. Another winner for Wolfgang Puck. Wonderful view from balcony. Entrees sized to share.

CHIN'S   ★★★★

Chinese   Expensive

3200 Las Vegas Blvd., S. (Fashion Show Mall); 733-8899
Strip Zone 1

Charlie Chin's at Arizona Charlie's, 740 S. Decatur Blvd.; 258-5200
Strip Zone 1

Fashion Show: Daily, noon–9:30 p.m.
Charlie Chin's: Daily, 4–9:30 p.m.
Comments: Multicourse dinners. Many restaurants try to copy
recipes; Chin's is lower-priced.

CHUNGKING EAST   ★★★½

Chinese buffet   Inexpensive

2710 E. Desert Inn Rd.; 693-6883
Zone 5

Lunch: Every day, 11:30 a.m.–5 p.m.
Dinner: Every day, 5–9 p.m.
Comments: Simple but comfortable; pleasing and clean. Dinner includes more seafood and meat; more dumplings and vegetables at lunch. Food is always fresh and hot. Latecomers get a 25% discount.

CIRCO (OSTERIA DEL)   ★★★½

Tuscan Italian   Moderate/Expensive

Bellagio; 693-8150
Strip Zone 1

Lunch & dinner: Daily, noon–midnight.
Comments: At once whimsical and vibrant—decor is pure fun. Casual, inviting, and comfortable.

COYOTE CAFÉ   ★★★★

Southwestern   Moderate/Expensive

MGM Grand; 891-7349
Strip Zone 1

Open: Daily, 9 a.m.–10:30 p.m.
Comments: All-day cafe plus dinner-only Grill Room. Flavorful, not palate-searing. Margarita bar with value-priced menu.

DIAMOND LIL'S ★★★

American   Moderate

Sam's Town, Boulder Hwy. at Flamingo Rd.; 456-7777
Southeast Zone 5

Dinner: Friday and Saturday, 5:30–10 p.m.; Sunday–Thursday, closed.
Comments: Turn-of-the-century decor. Fine dining, moderate prices.

DIVE! ★★★½

American   Moderate

Fashion Show Mall; 369-3483
Strip Zone 1

Lunch & dinner: Sunday–Thursday, 11:30 a.m.–10 p.m.; Friday and Saturday, 11:30 a.m.–11 p.m.
Comments: Submarine-themed with porthole windows, special effects. Sublime desserts. Children's and adult parties a specialty.

DRAI'S ★★★★½

California-Continental   Moderate/Expensive

Barbary Coast Hotel; 737-0555
Strip Zone 1

Dinner: Sunday–Thursday, 6–10 p.m.; Friday and Saturday, 6–11:30 p.m.
Comments: Original art, mostly nudes. Expertly cooked fish. Live jazz from 8:30 p.m. to closing Friday and Saturday in lounge.

EMERIL'S NEW ORLEANS FISH HOUSE ★★★★½

Contemporary New Orleans   Expensive

MGM Grand; 891-7777
Strip Zone 1

Lunch: Daily, 11 a.m.–2:30 p.m.
Dinner: Daily, 5:30–10:30 p.m.
Oyster Bar/Cafe: Daily, 11 a.m.–10:30 p.m.
Comments: A bit of New Orleans. "Tasting" dinners offer small portions of many dishes.

FELLINI'S   ★★★½

Regional Italian/Provençal   Moderate/Expensive

5555 W. Charleston Blvd.; 870-9999
Southwest Zone 3

Dinner: Monday–Thursday, 5–10 p.m.; Friday and Saturday, 5–11 p.m.; Sunday, closed.
Comments: European-style dessert table. Breads made on site. Live piano music. Free limousine on request.

FERRARO'S RESTAURANT & LOUNGE   ★★★½

Italian   Moderate/Expensive

5900 W. Flamingo Rd.; 364-5300
Southwest Zone 3

Dinner: Daily, 5–11 p.m.
Comments: Roman-style dining room. Light menu available. Strolling guitarist.

FIORE ★★★★

Continental   Moderate/Expensive

Rio, 3700 W. Flamingo Rd.; 252-7777
Strip Zone 1

Dinner: Daily, 5–11 p.m.
Comments: Menu changes every seven to ten days. Cigar terrace for smokers.

FORTUNE ★★★★

Chinese   Moderate/Expensive

Rio, Valley View and Flamingo; 247-7923
Strip Zone 1

Dinner: Daily, 6–11 p.m.
Comments: Stunning restaurant; museum-quality art and arti-facts. Live seafood is expensive (ask prices); Santa Barbara shrimp are worth the cost.

FUJI ★★★

Japanese   Inexpensive/Moderate

3430 E. Tropicana Ave.; 435-8838
Southeast Zone 5

Open: Daily, 4:30–10:30 p.m.; Sunday, closes at 10 p.m.
Comments: Small family-style restaurant. Basic Japanese fare is available. Children welcome.

GARDUNO'S CHILI PACKING CO. ★★★½

Mexican   Inexpensive/Moderate

Fiesta Hotel, 2400 N. Rancho Dr.; 631-7000
Northwest Zone 4

Brunch: Sunday, 10 a.m.–3 p.m.
Lunch & dinner: Sunday, 10 a.m.–10 p.m.; Monday–Thursday,
11 a.m.–10 p.m.; Friday and Saturday, 11 a.m.–11 p.m.
Comments: Hatch, N.M., chiles used exclusively. Guacamole
prepared tableside.

GATSBY'S ★★★★

Asian-French/California-style   Expensive

MGM Grand; 891-7777
Strip Zone 1

Dinner: Tuesday–Saturday, 6–11 p.m.; Sunday and Monday,
closed.
Comments: Prix fixe three-, four-, and five-course dinners. Dinner and EFX! show package ($115) includes preferred show seat-
ing.

GRAPE STREET ★★★½

American bistro and wine bar   Inexpensive/Moderate

7501 W. Lake Mead Blvd. (Summerhill Plaza); 228-9463
North Zone 4

Lunch & dinner: Sunday and Tuesday–Thursday, 11 a.m.–10
p.m.; Friday and Saturday, 11 a.m.–11 p.m.; Monday, closed. Dinner specials from 4 p.m.
Comments: Delightful. Always busy. Outdoor patio. About 50
wines available by the glass. Takeout counter.

HABIB'S   ★★★½

Persian/Middle Eastern   Moderate

4750 W. Sahara Ave., Sahara Pavilion; 870-0860
Southwest Zone 3

Lunch: Monday–Saturday, 11:30 a.m.–3 p.m.
Dinner: Monday–Saturday, 5–10 p.m.; Sunday, closed.
Comments: City's only Persian restaurant. Mist-cooled patio.
Delicious dishes with unfamiliar names; menu has photos.

HUGO'S CELLAR   ★★★½²

American   Expensive

Four Queens Hotel; 385-4011
Downtown Zone 2

Dinner: Daily, 5:30–11 p.m.
Comments: Popular but overpriced. Packed on weekends.

IL FORNAIO   ★★★

Italian   Moderate/Moderately Expensive

New York–New York; 740-6969
Strip Zone 1

Lunch & dinner: Sunday–Thursday, 11:30 a.m.–11 p.m.; Friday and Saturday, 11:30 a.m.–12:30 a.m.; Saturday and Sunday, open at 9 a.m. for breakfast.
Comments: Upscale, upbeat. Remarkable breads, homemade pastas. Outdoor patio. Off-hours more relaxing.

ISIS   ★★★½

Continental	Expensive

Luxor; 262-4773
Strip Zone 1

Dinner: Daily, 6–11 p.m.
Comments: Replicas of pharaonic statues. Egyptian artifacts separate booths. Harpist at entrance.

JERUSALEM   ★★½

Glatt Kosher	Moderate/Inexpensive

Plaza de Vegas, 1305 Vegas Valley Dr.
(East of Maryland Parkway); 696-1644
Southeast Zone 5

Lunch & dinner: Sunday–Thursday, 10 a.m.–9 p.m.; Friday, 10 a.m.–3:30 p.m.; Saturday, closed. Same menu.
Comments: Best of city's few kosher restaurants. Large portions.

KATHY'S SOUTHERN COOKING   ★★★

American	Inexpensive

6407 Mountain Vista St.; 433-1005
Southeast Zone 5

Lunch & dinner: Tuesday–Sunday, 11 a.m.–8 p.m.; Monday, closed. Same menu.
Comments: Authentic dishes from Mississippi and Louisiana. Park in shopping center and walk to Mountain Vista Street.

KOKOMO'S ★★★★

Seafood/Steak   Expensive

The Mirage; 791-7111
Strip Zone 1

Breakfast: Thursday–Sunday, 8–10:30 a.m.
Lunch: Daily, 11 a.m.–2:30 p.m.
Dinner: Daily, 5:30–11 p.m.
Comments: Magnificent tropical decor. Peaceful and romantic; one of Las Vegas's best-kept secrets.

LAWRY'S THE PRIME RIB ★★★½²

American   Expensive

4043 Howard Hughes Pwy.; 893-2223
Strip Zone 1

Dinner: Sunday–Thursday, 5–10 p.m.; Friday and Saturday, 5–11 p.m.
Comments: In a city filled with prime-rib deals, Lawry's survives as the ultimate temple of beefdom.

LINDO MICHOACAN ★★★

Mexican   Moderate

2655 E. Desert Inn Rd.; 735-6828
Southeast Zone 5

Lunch & dinner: Monday–Thursday, 11 a.m.–10 p.m.; Friday–Sunday, 9:30 a.m.–11 p.m. Same menu day and evening; lunch specials.
Comments: Neighborhood cantina. Lunch buffet Monday–Friday, brunch buffet weekends.

LOTUS OF SIAM   ★★★

Thai   Moderate

953 E. Sahara Ave., Commercial Center; 735-3033
Strip Zone 1

Lunch: Monday–Friday buffet, 11:30 a.m.–2:30 p.m. and regular menu.
Dinner: Daily, 4:30–10 p.m.
Comments: Small but good lunch buffet. Vegetarian menu available.

MAGNOLIA ROOM   ★★★½

Italian/Greek/American   Moderate

Jerry's Nugget; 399-3000
North Las Vegas Zone 4

Brunch: Sunday, 9 a.m.–3 p.m.
Dinner: Wednesday–Sunday, 3–10 p.m.; Monday and Tuesday, closed.
Comments: A real find. The food isn't epicurean, but it doesn't pretend to be. Early-bird dinners are a fine value.

MAKINO SUSHI RESTAURANT   ★★★★

Japanese   Inexpensive/Moderate

Renaissance Center, Decatur near Flamingo; 889-4477
Zone 3

Lunch: 11:30 a.m.–2:30 p.m. Monday–Friday, 11:30 a.m.–3 p.m. Saturday, Sunday, and holidays.
Dinner: 5:30–9 p.m. Monday–Thursday, 5:30–10 p.m. Friday; 5–10 p.m. Saturday; 5–9 p.m. Sunday and holidays.
Comments: You'll not find a more appealing array of foods. The sushi alone is worth more than what it costs for this no-limits Japanese feast.

MAMOUNIA ★★★½

Moroccan   Moderate

4632 S. Maryland Pkwy.; 597-0092
Strip Zone I

Dinner: Daily, 5:30–11 p.m.
Comments: Simulated desert tent with costumed servers. Belly dancers undulate. Most dishes served without silverware.

MANHATTAN ★★★½

Italian   Moderate/Expensive

2600 E. Flamingo Rd.; 737-5000
Strip Zone I

Dinner: Daily, 5 p.m.–1 a.m.
Comments: Bar has late-night menu. Good food even better when chef/owner P.J. is in the kitchen. Free limousine on request.

MARRAKECH ★★★

Moroccan   Moderate

3900 Paradise Rd.; 736-7655
Strip Zone I

Dinner: Daily, 5:30–11 p.m.
Comments: Simulated desert tent with costumed servers. No silverware. Las Vegas version of Moroccan food. Belly dancing is often intrusive.

MAYFLOWER CUISINIER   ★★★★¹/₂²

Chinese/French   Moderate/Expensive

4750 W. Sahara Ave.; 870-8432
Southwest Zone 3

Lunch: Monday–Friday, 11 a.m.–2:30 p.m.
Dinner: Monday–Thursday, 5–9:30 p.m.; Friday and Saturday,
5–10:30 p.m.; Sunday, closed.
Comments: Two levels; mezzanine more private. Mist-cooled patio. Excellent fusion of Chinese and other cuisines.

MICHAEL'S   ★★★★

Very Continental   Expensive

Barbary Coast Hotel; 737-7111
Strip Zone 1

Dinner: Daily, two seatings at 6:30 and 9:30 p.m.
Comments: Luxurious, rococo room. Complimentary after-dinner sweets. If you're staying on the Strip, the casino can help with a reservation.

MONTE CARLO   ★★★★¹/₂

Continental   Expensive

Desert Inn; 733-4444
Strip Zone 1

Dinner: Thursday–Monday, 6–11 p.m.; Tuesday and Wednesday, closed.
Comments: Beautiful, romantic room. Waiters make a major production of flaming dishes. Allow three hours for meal.

MORTONI'S   ★★★½

Italian, California-style   Moderate/Expensive

Hard Rock Hotel, Harmon Ave. and Paradise Rd.; 693-5000
Strip Zone I

Dinner: Daily, 5–11 p.m.
Comments: Small but choice menu using natural ingredients and organic produce. Despite restaurant's location, music isn't intrusive.

MORTON'S   ★★★½

Steak   Expensive

3200 Las Vegas Blvd., S. (Fashion Show Mall); 893-0703
Strip Zone I

Dinner: Monday–Thursday, 5:30–11 p.m.; Friday and Saturday, 5–11 p.m; Sunday, 5–10 p.m.
Comments: Men's club atmosphere; cigar smoking encouraged. Dessert soufflés disappoint; choose pastry or the gorgeous berries.

NAPA   ★★★★★

Contemporary French   Expensive

Rio, Valley View and Flamingo; 252-7777
Strip Zone I

Dinner: Wednesday–Sunday, 6–11 p.m.; Monday and Tuesday, closed.
Comments: Ambience for women, but men comfortable. Superb tasting room; modest prices, 250 wines by the glass.

NEROS   ★★★★

Contemporary American   Expensive

Caesars Palace Hotel; 731-7731
Strip Zone 1

Dinner: Sunday–Thursday, 5:30–10 p.m.; Friday and Saturday, 5:30–10:30 p.m.
Comments: Understated elegance. Splendid desserts. Menus change regularly.

NOODLES   ★★★½

Asian   Moderate

Bellagio; 693-7111
Strip Zone 1

Open: Every day, 11 a.m.–3 a.m.
Comments: Small space with open kitchen, wall of artifacts, and the hustle and bustle of an authentic noodle kitchen. A favorite stop for Bellagio's Asian clientele.

NORTH BEACH CAFÉ   ★★★½

Italian   Moderate

2605 S. Decatur Blvd.; 247-9530
Southwest Zone 3

Lunch: Monday–Saturday, 11:30 a.m.–4:30 p.m.
Dinner: Monday–Friday, 5–10 p.m.; Saturday, 5–10:30 p.m.; Sunday, 5–9 p.m.
Comments: Cheerful. Patio service. Among nice touches is unusual empanadas Argentinas appetizer.

OLIVES ★★★★

American/Mediterranean   Moderate/Expensive

Bellagio; 693-7223
Strip Zone 1

Lunch & dinner: Sunday–Thursday, 11 a.m.–midnight; Friday
and Saturday, 11 a.m.–1 a.m.
Comments: An outdoor patio with a view of the lake. Menu
changes regularly. Wonderful sandwiches at lunch. Bears no re-
semblance to the Boston original, but does have the same warmth
and expert staff.

PALACE COURT ★★★★★

Continental   Expensive

Caesars Palace; 731-7110
Strip Zone 1

Dinner: Daily, seatings every half-hour from 6 to 10 p.m.; none
at 6:30 or 8 p.m.
Comments: Superb dining amid elegance. Early patrons watch
the sunset. Pianist in bar. Tasting dinners a specialty.

THE PALM ★★★★

Steak   Expensive

The Forum Shops at Caesars; 732-7256
Strip Zone 1

Lunch & dinner: Daily, 11:30 a.m.–10:30 p.m.
Comments: Caters to celebrities. Very busy. Insist on dining
room; rear banquet room is drab and noisy.

PAMPLEMOUSSE   ★★★½

Continental/French   Expensive

400 E. Sahara Ave.; 733-2066
Strip Zone 1

Dinner: Tuesday–Sunday, 6–9:30 p.m.; Monday, closed.
Comments: Attractive wine cellar. No menu; ask waiter for prices.

PASTA PIRATE   ★★★½

Seafood/Pasta   Moderate

California Hotel, 12 Ogden Ave.; 385-1222
Downtown Zone 2

Dinner: Daily, 5:30–11 p.m.
Comments: Small, waterfront-motif restaurant. Imaginative menu. Consistently good food. Entrees include glass of wine.

PEKING MARKET   ★★★½

Chinese   Moderate

Flamingo Hilton; 733-3111
Strip Zone 1

Dinner: Wednesday–Sunday, 5:30–11 p.m.; Monday and Tuesday, closed.
Comments: Contemporary Chinese; authentic art and antiques. Well-priced family-style dinners. Extensive regional Chinese menu.

PHILIPS SUPPER HOUSE ★★★

American/Prime Rib   Moderate

4545 W. Sahara Ave.; 873-5222
Southwest Zone 3

Dinner: Daily, 4:30–10:30 p.m.
Comments: Victorian, bay-windowed home. Hearty dinners. Very good early bird specials.

PICASSO ★★★★★

French with Spanish influence   Expensive

Bellagio; 693-7223
Strip Zone I

Dinner: Sunday–Tuesday and Thursday, 6–10 p.m.; Friday and Saturday, 6–11 p.m.; Wednesday, closed.
Comments: Arguably the most beautiful dining room in Las Vegas—original Picasso artworks, wall of windows with view of dancing fountains. Grand yet unpretentious.

PIERO'S ★★★★½

Italian   Expensive

355 Convention Center Dr.; 369-2305
Strip Zone I

Dinner: Daily, 5:30–9 p.m.
Comments: Celebrities, sports figures, and Las Vegas powerbrokers dine here. Champagnes and $400 bottles of Montrachet are the norm.

PRIME   ★★★★

Steakhouse   Expensive

Bellagio; 693-8484
Strip Zone 1

Dinner: Daily, 5:30–11 p.m.
Comments: Dazzling setting seldom seen for a steakhouse—plenty of original art. It's hard to resist this rare steakhouse.

RAINFOREST CAFÉ   ★★★½

American   Moderate

MGM Grand; 891-8580
Strip Zone 1

Breakfast: Daily, 7–10:15 a.m.
Lunch & dinner: Daily, 10:30 a.m. until closing; Monday–Thursday and Sunday, until 11 p.m.; Friday and Saturday, until 1 a.m.
Comments: Faux tropical paradise. Better food than at most themed-restaurants plus wonderful concept. Ask about free safari tours.

RANGE STEAKHOUSE   ★★★½

American   Expensive

Harrah's; 369-5000
Strip Zone 1

Dinner: Sunday–Thursday, 5:30–10:30 p.m.; Friday and Saturday, 5:30–11:30 p.m.
Comments: Every table has a splendid view. Harrah's has changed dramatically, and the Range exemplifies the new direction.

REDWOOD BAR & GRILL   ★★★½

American/Prime Rib   Moderate

California Hotel, 12 Ogden Ave.; 385-1222
Downtown Zone 2

Dinner: Daily, 5:30–11 p.m.
Comments: Country English decor. Pianist nightly. Succulent prime rib in generous portions.

RICARDO'S   ★★★½

Mexican   Moderate

4930 W. Flamingo Rd.; 871-7119
Southwest Zone 3

2380 E. Tropicana Ave.; 798-4515
Southeast Zone 5

MGM Grand; 736-4970
Strip Zone 1

Lunch & dinner: Same menu all day, all locations. West Flamingo Road and East Tropicana Avenue: Friday and Saturday, 11 a.m.–11 p.m.; Sunday–Thursday, 11 a.m.–10 p.m. MGM Grand: daily, 11 a.m.–11 p.m.
Comments: MGM Grand branch especially colorful. Lunch buffet Monday–Saturday at West Flamingo and East Tropicana locations.

RISTORANTE ITALIANO   ★★★½

Italian   Expensive

Riviera Hotel; 734-5110
Strip Zone 1

Dinner: Friday–Tuesday, 5:30–10:30 p.m.; Wednesday and Thursday, closed.
Comments: A favorite of stars performing at the hotel. Contemporary plus classic Italian dishes. Private dining room available.

ROSEWOOD GRILLE   ★★★½

Lobster/Steak   Expensive

3339 Las Vegas Blvd., S.; 792-9099
Strip Zone I

Dinner: Daily, 4:30–11:30 p.m.
Comments: Always busy, but retains Old World charm. Lobsters up to 25 pounds; typically $17 to $22 per pound.

RUTH'S CHRIS STEAK HOUSE   ★★★★

Steak   Expensive

3900 Paradise Rd.; 791-7011
Strip Zone I

4561 W. Flamingo Rd.; 248-7011
Southwest Zone 5

Lunch: Paradise: Monday–Friday, 11 a.m.–4:30 p.m.
Dinner: Paradise: daily, 4:30–10:30 p.m.; Flamingo: daily, 4:30 p.m.–3 a.m. (kitchen closes 2:30 a.m.).
Comments: Wines include $100 to $300 bottles. Meal for two can be steep; portions large enough to share.

SAIGON   ★★★

Vietnamese   Inexpensive/Moderate

4251 W. Sahara Ave.; 362-9978
Southwest Zone 3

Lunch & dinner: Daily, 10 a.m.–10 p.m.; lunch specials, 10 a.m.–3 p.m.
Comments: Vietnamese headquarters of Las Vegas. Interesting food; beware hot peppers! Quality inconsistent, but at these prices, it's worth a try.

SAM WOO BAR-B-Q   ★★★

Chinese Barbecue   Inexpensive

Chinatown Mall, 4215 Spring Mountain Rd.; 368-7628
Southwest Zone 3

Lunch & dinner: Daily, 10 a.m.–5 a.m. Takeout barbecue shop:
daily, 10 a.m.–10 p.m.
Comments: One of the best values in a town filled with them.
Very little English spoken, but menu is in English. Service may
be brusque.

SAMBA GRILL   ★★★★

Brazilian steakhouse   Moderate

Mirage; 791-7111
Strip Zone 1

Dinner: Every night, 5:30–11 p.m.
Comments: Vibrant colors. Continuous guitar music a lovely extra. A terrific new restaurant with prices right out of Old Las Vegas.

SEASONS   ★★★★

Continental   Expensive

Bally's; 739-4111
Strip Zone 1

Dinner: Tuesday–Saturday, 6–11 p.m.; Sunday and Monday,
closed.
Comments: Exquisite room. Menu includes lighter, healthful
dishes; fare changes quarterly.

SFUZZI LAS VEGAS   ★★★

Italian   Moderate

Fashion Show Mall; 699-5777
Strip Zone I

Brunch & lunch: Sunday, noon–4 p.m. Lunch: Monday–Saturday, 11 a.m.–4 p.m.
Dinner: Daily, 4 p.m.–midnight.
Comments: Sfuzzi (FOO-zee—slang for fun food) considers itself an Italian bistro, but decor is spectacular. Walls of windows
for people-watching.

SHALIMAR   ★★★½

Indian   Moderate/Expensive

3900 Paradise Rd.; 796-0302
Strip Zone I

2605 S. Decatur Blvd.; 252-8320
Southwest Zone 3

Lunch: Monday–Friday buffet, 11:30 a.m.–2 p.m.; Saturday and
Sunday, closed.
Dinner: Daily, 5:30–10:30 p.m.
Comments: Tandoori oven produces delicious breads and skin-
less chicken in minutes. Curries spiced to taste; $10 buffet lunch.

SIR GALAHAD'S   ★★★½

Prime rib   Moderate

Excalibur; 597-7777
Strip Zone I

Dinner: Sunday–Thursday, 5–10 p.m.; Friday and Saturday,
5–11 p.m.
Comments: English castle; Arthurian-costumed servers. Prime
rib sliced tableside.

SPAGO ★★★★★

American   Moderate/Expensive

The Forum Shops at Caesars Palace; 369-6300
Strip Zone 1

Lunch & dinner: Cafe: daily, 11 a.m.–11 p.m.
Dinner: Restaurant: daily, 6–10 p.m.
Comments: Chef Wolfgang Puck offers the best staff and ingredients. Noisy, but people-watching is terrific. Signature pizzas, exquisite appetizers.

THE STEAK HOUSE ★★★½

Steak   Moderate

Circus Circus; 734-0410
Strip Zone 1

Dinner: Daily, 5 p.m.–midnight.
Comments: Despite children running around the lobby, restaurant is adult and food wonderful.

STEFANO'S ★★★★

Southern Italian   Expensive

Golden Nugget; 385-7111
Downtown Zone 2

Dinner: Sunday–Thursday, 6–10:30 p.m.; Friday and Saturday, 5:30–10:30 p.m.
Comments: Staff sings Italian classics; you will, too. Dishes have flair. A happy experience.

SWISS CAFÉ   ★★★½

European   Moderate

3175 E. Tropicana Ave.; 454-2270
Southeast Zone 5

Lunch: Monday–Friday, 11 a.m.–2:30 p.m.
Dinner: Monday–Saturday, 5–10 p.m.; Sunday, closed.
Comments: Old World charm. Entrees include handmade apple strudel. Specials on blackboard.

TERRAZZA   ★★★★½

Italian   Expensive

Caesars Palace; 731-7110
Strip Zone 1

Dinner: Daily, 5:30–11 p.m.
Comments: Italian rustic. Patio offers splendid view of Palace Tower and swimming pools.

TERU SUSHI   ★★★½

Sushi   Moderate/Expensive

700 E. Sahara Ave.; 734-6655
Strip Zone 1

Dinner: Monday–Saturday, 5–11 p.m.; Sunday, closed.
Comments: High-quality sushi is the best and priced accordingly. Portions small; hearty appetites will require many dishes (can get costly).

THE TILLERMAN ★★★½

Seafood   Moderate/Expensive

2245 E. Flamingo Rd.; 731-4036
Southeast Zone 5

Dinner: Daily, 5–11 p.m.
Comments: Very popular. Over ten types of fresh fish daily. Airy dining room with balcony seating.

TOKYO ★★★½

Japanese/Sushi   Moderate

953 E. Sahara Ave., Commercial Center; 735-7070
Strip Zone 1

Dinner: Daily, 5–10 p.m.
Comments: Family-run; very popular. Hibachi grills for cooking your own dinner.

TOP OF THE WORLD ★★★½

American   Expensive

Stratosphere Tower, 2000 Las Vegas Blvd., South; 380-7711
Strip Zone 1

Dinner: Sunday–Thursday, 5–11 p.m.; Friday and Saturday, 6 p.m.–midnight.
Comments: Without question, the most beautiful view of the city. Revolving restaurant; no bad seating. $15 food minimum.

TRE VISI/LA SCALA ★★★

Italian　　　　　　　　　　　　　　　Moderate/Expensive

MGM Grand; 891-1111 (La Scala), 891-7777 (Tre Visi)
Strip Zone 1

Breakfast: Tre Visi: 8–11 a.m.
Lunch: 11 a.m.–3 p.m.
Dinner: La Scala: daily, 5:30–10 p.m. (extended when warranted); Tre Visi: 3–11 p.m.
Comments: Exceptional wine list; 1,000 bottles in cellar. Large, but highest standards intact. Booths in La Scala dining room emulate boxes at Milan opera.

VENETIAN ★★★½

Italian　　　　　　　　　　　　　　　Moderate/Expensive

3713 W. Sahara Ave.; 876-4190
Southwest Zone 3

Open: Daily, 24 hours (dinner starts at 4 p.m.)
Comments: Updated dining room. Very popular sautéed greens and marinated pork neckbones are unique to Venetian.

VIVA MERCADO'S ★★★½

Mexican　　　　　　　　　　　　　　　Moderate

6182 W. Flamingo Rd.; 871-8826
Southwest Zone 3

Town Center (adjacent to Barley's Sunset); 435-6200
Southeast Zone 5

Lunch & dinner: Sunday–Thursday, 11 a.m.–9:30 p.m.; Friday and Saturday, 11 a.m.–10:30 p.m. Same menu lunch and dinner.
Comments: Canola oil used in cooking. Cheese can be eliminated from any dish. Lunch specials. Saturday and Sunday sangria brunch.

VOODOO CAFE & LOUNGE   ★★★½

Creole/Cajun   Moderate/Expensive

Rio, Valley View and Flamingo; 252-7777
Strip Zone 1

Open: Daily, 11 a.m.–3 a.m.
Lounge: Daily, 5–11 p.m.
Comments: Spectacular view of Strip from atop one of city's tallest buildings. Bartenders do tricks while mixing drinks.

WOLFGANG PUCK CAFÉ   ★★★½

American   Moderate

MGM Grand; 891-3019
Strip Zone 1

Lunch & dinner: Sunday–Thursday, 11 a.m.–11 p.m.; Friday and Saturday, 8 a.m.–midnight.
Comments: Sidewalk cafe allows people-watching over MGM Grand's casino. Slow service and inconsistent quality at peak hours.

Index

Adult entertainment, 118, 120, 121, 124–25
Adventuredome, 148
Airport
  arrival at, 15, 17
  distances to lodgings, 27–29
  map of, 7
American Superstars, 94–95
Aquatic shows, 98–99, 112
Arrival and orientation, 15–22
  by airport, 15, 17
  by car, 15
  local systems and protocols, 18–21
  rental cars, 15, 17–18
  visitor guides, 12–13
Auto collection, 153

Baccarat
  best casino for, 136
  house advantage in, 128–29
  lessons on, 133
  rules of, 142–43
Bars and lounges, 82, 117–23
Betting, sports, 136
Bingo, 136, 142–43
Blackjack, 130
  best casino for, 135
  double exposure 21, 134
  house advantage in, 128–29
  lessons on, 133
  rules of, 142–43
  single-deck, 134
Boulder Highway, 11, 34
Bowling, best hotels for, 77
Buffets, 76, 156–59
Bus service, 18
Business travelers, 25, 42–44. *See also* Convention Center

Cabs. *See* Taxis
Calendar, for shows, 82–83

Car(s)
  rental of, 15, 17–18
  sneak routes for, 34–36
Card games. *See also* Blackjack; Poker
  baccarat, 133, 142–43
  lessons on, 133
Caribbean Stud, 133, 136, 142
Cashman Field Center, 43
Casinos. *See also* Gambling
  ambiance of, 45
  democracy in, 45
  in hotels, 45–65, 73–75
  Internet information on, 13
  large vs. small, 25, 27
  restaurants in, 155
Catch a Rising Star, 115
Celebrity headliners, 81, 89–93
Chance, games of, 129–32
Cheating, in gambling, 124
Chicago (show), 96–97
Children
  activities for, 21–22, 153
    MGM Grand Adventures Park, 55–57, 146–47
    shows, 89
  gambling restrictions and, 21
  lodging for, 56
Circus shows, 97–98, 98–99, 105–6
Cirque du Soleil
  Mystere, 97–98
  "*O*," 98–99
Clark County, map of, 16
Clothes, 14, 85
Clubs
  comedy, 82, 86, 114–17
  night life, 117–23
  slot, 140–41
Cocktail shows, 84
Comedy clubs and shows, 82, 86, 114–17

Comedy Max, 115–16
Comedy Stop, 116
Commission, on gambling winnings, 129
Commuting, 27–29
Compulsive gambling, 136–37
Convenience chart, for distances between locations, 27–29
Convention Center, 43
    distances from, 27–29, 30, 44
    lodging convenience and, 25
    parking at, 43–44
    transportation to, 44
Conventions
    crowds during, 15
    lodgings for, 42–44
Coupon books, 134
Craps
    best casino for, 135
    crapless, 134
    double odds in, 134
    house advantage in, 128–29
    lessons on, 133
    rules of, 142–43
    triple odds in, 134
Crazy Girls, 99–100
Crime, 123–25
Crowds, avoidance of, 15, 37
Customs, local, 18–21

Dancing, nightspots for, 117–23
Dealers, tipping of, 20
Desert Inn, 90
Dice games. *See* Craps
Dining. *See* Restaurants
Dinner shows, 84, 95–96
Discounts
    for lodging, 39–41
    for Players Club, 40
    at restaurants, 161–62
Double exposure 21, 134
Downtown
    commuting to/from, 27–29
    Fremont Street Experience, 153
    lodging in, 23, 25–29, 31
    map of, 8, 26

Dress recommendations, 14, 85
Drinks
    at bars and lounges, 117–23
    at shows, 88

Eating. *See* Restaurants
EFX, 101
Enter the Night, 101–2
Entertainment. *See also* Shows
    adult, 118, 120, 121, 124–25
    night life, 117–23
Evening at La Cage, An, 102–3
Evening at the Improv, An, 116
Excursions, for children, 22
Exercise equipment, best hotels for, 77–78
Exit Information Guide, 41

Flatley, Michael, Lord of the Dance, 108–9
Folies Bergere (The Best of), 103
Forever Plaid, 104–5
Free attractions, 153
Fremont Street Experience, 153
Funbooks, 134

Gamblers Anonymous, 137
Gambler's Book Club, 133
Gambling, 126–43. *See also* Casinos
    attitudes in, 136–37
    best casinos for, vs. game type, 134–36
    cheating in, 124
    compulsive, 136–37
    disciplined approach to, 130–32
    games of chance and skill in, 130
    games of chance in, 129–32
    house advantage in, 127–29
    house commission in, 129
    jargon of, 134
    law of averages in, 129–32
    lessons on, 132–34
    marketing strategies for, 126
    protocol for, 19
    reference works on, 133
    restrictions for children, 21

Gambling *(Continued)*
  rules of, 137–43
  short run vs. long run results of,
    126–27
  strategies for, 130–32
  supplies for, 145
Gans, Danny, "The Man of Many
  Voices," 100
Geographic zones, 5–12
"Glitter Gulch," 23
Golf, best hotels for, 77
Great Radio City Spectacular, The,
  105
Green Valley, lodging in, 34
Guests, invited to shows, 85

Half-price programs, for lodging,
  40
High rollers, 45
Hoover Dam, tours of, 154
Hotels. *See* Lodging
House advantage, in gambling,
  127–29

Ice skating, facilities for, 77
Imagine (show), 105–6
Impersonator shows, 82
  American Superstars, 94–95
  Evening at La Cage, An, 102–3
  Legends in Concert, 108
Impressionists, 100
Improv, The (Harrah's), *Evening at
  the Improv, An*, 116
Information, 12–13
Internet, information on, 13
Invited guests, to shows, 85
Irish dance shows, 108–9

Jogging, 77
Jousting show, 113–14
Jubilee!, 106–7

Keno
  best casino for, 136
  house advantage in, 128–29
  lessons on, 133

  rules of, 142–43
  tipping in, 20

Lake Mead, 153–54
Lance Burton: Master Magician,
  107–8
Las Vegas Convention and Visitors
  Authority, 82–83
Las Vegas Convention Center. *See*
  Convention Center
Law of averages, in games of chance,
  129–32
Legends in Concert, 108
Leisure, lodgings ratings for, 73–78
Lessons, on gambling, 132–34
Let it Ride, 133, 136, 142
Liberace Museum, 153
Lied Discovery Museum, 153
Light shows, 153
Line passes, to shows, 85
Lion habitat, 148
Lodging, 23–80
  basic choices in, 23–27
  best deals in, 36–39, 72–73
  Boulder Highway, 34
  for business travelers, 25, 42–44
  with casinos, 45–65, 73–75
  with children, 56
  comfort zones of, 45–65
  convenience chart for, 27–29
  near Convention Center, 43, 44
  convention rates for, 42–44
  costs of, 67–73
  discounts for, 39–41
  Downtown, 23, 25–29, 31
  family-oriented, 56
  Green Valley, 34
  half-price programs for, 40
  large vs. small facilities, 25, 27
  maps for, 26, 30, 33, 35
  motels, 67
  North Las Vegas, 34
  package deals for, 38–39, 42
  parking at, 25
  problems with, 39
  rating/ranking of

best deals, 36–39
leisure, recreation, and services, 73–78
overall rating list, 78–80
room quality, 67–71
reservations for, 36–41
for business travelers, 42–44
cancelled, 39
hotel-sponsored packages, 41
options for, 37
from Players Club, 40
problems with, 39
room allocation practices in, 36
services for, 41
timing of, 38
from tour operators, 39–40, 42
from travel agents, 38–39
from wholesalers, 39–40, 42
services of, rating of, 73–78
show ticket sales in, 84
small vs. large, 25, 27
sneak routes into, 34–36
Strip, 23–25, 27–28, 30–34
near Strip, 34
suite hotels, 66
tipping for, 20
unassociated with convention room blocks, 42
Lord of the Dance, 108–9
Lounges and bars, 82, 117–23

McCarran Airport. *See* Airport
Magic shows, 112–13
Caesars Magical Empire, 95–96
Lance Burton: Master Magician, 107–8
Siegfried & Roy, 109–11
Spellbound, 111
Maître d'
seating at shows, 85–87
tipping of, 20, 87–88
Malls, 144–46
"Man of Many Voices, The," 100
Maps. *See* List of Illustrations on page vii
Maxim, 115–16

Medieval pageant, *Tournament of Kings*, 113–14
Megabucks slots, 134
MGM Grand Adventures Theme Park, 55–57, 146–47
Michael Flatley's Lord of the Dance, 108–9
Motels. *See* Lodging
Museums, 153
Music
in nightspots, 117–23
rock concerts, 90–91
Mystere (Cirque du Soleil), 97–98

Natural attractions, 153–54
Natural history Museum, 153
Nevada, map of, 2
News stand, 21
Night life, 117–23
North Las Vegas, 10, 34
Nude shows, 121

"O," Cirque du Soleil's, 98–99
One-arm bandits. *See* Slot machines
Orientation. *See* Arrival and orientation
Outdoor recreation, 153–54

Package deals, 38–39
for convention attendees, 42
hotel-sponsored, 41
Players Club, 40
Pai gow poker, 133, 136, 142–43
Parking
at Convention Center, 43–44
at lodgings, 25
for shows, 86
tipping for, 20
Passes, to shows, 85
Players Club, reservations through, 40
Poker, 130
best casinos for, 136
lessons on, 133
pai gow, 133, 136, 142–43
video, 128–29, 135, 141–42

Production shows, 82, 93–114
  calendar for, 82–83
  hit parade of, 94
  profiles of, alphabetical listing of,
    93–114
  seating for, 85–88
Prostitution, 124
Protocols, local, 18–21
Publications, 12–13
  on gambling, 133
  show calendar, 82–83

Race betting, best casino for, 136
Radio City Music Hall show, 105
Recreation
  golf, 77
  lodgings ratings for, 73–78
Rental, cars, 15, 17–18
Reservations
  for lodging. *See* Lodging, reserva-
    tions for
  for rental cars, 17
  for shows, 83–84, 85–86. *See also*
    specific show and showroom
Rest rooms, at showrooms, 88
Restaurants, 155–209
  alphabetical listing of, 174–209
  best, 163–74
  best hotels for, 76
  buffets, 156–59
  in casinos, 155
  cuisine types in, 165–74
  dinner shows at, 84
  discounts at, 155–56, 161–62
  new, 162–63
  tipping in, 20
Rides, at attractions, 146–53
Riviera Comedy Club, 116–17
Roller coasters, 152–53
Romantic atmosphere, 76, 121
Rooms. *See* Lodging
Roulette
  best casino for, 136
  house advantage in, 128–29
  lessons on, 133
  rules of, 142–43

Running (jogging), best hotels for,
  77

Scandia Family Fun Center, 153
Seasons for visiting, 13–15, 37
Sex in Las Vegas, 118, 120, 121,
  124–25
Shopping, 77, 144–46
Shows, 81–117
  aquatic, 98–99, 112
  calendar for, 82–83
  celebrity headliner, 81, 89–93
  changeable nature of, 82
  for children, 89
  circus, 97–98, 98–99, 105–6
  cocktail, 84
  comedy, 82, 86, 114–17
  dinner, 84, 95–96
  dress for, 85
  drink service at, 88
  early vs. late, 84
  hit parade of, 94
  impersonator, 82, 94–95, 102–3,
    108
  invited guests to, 85
  late vs. early, 84
  line passes for, 85
  long-term engagements, 81
  lounge, 82
  magic. *See* Magic shows
  medieval tournament, 113–14
  nude, 121
  parking for, 86
  prices of, 83
  production. *See* Production shows
  reservations for, 83–86. *See also*
    specific show and showroom
  rest rooms at, 88
  seating at, 85–88
  selection of, 88–89
  strip, 124
  taxes on, 83
  ticket sales for, 83–84
  tipping at, 87–88
  topless, 124–25
  transportation to, 86

types of, 81–82
for under-21 crowd, 89
without reservations, 84
Siegfried & Roy, 109–11
Sight-seeing, 146–54
Skating, best hotels for, 77
Slot machines, 45
best casino for, 135
house advantage in, 128–29
loose, 134
megabucks, 134
rules for, 137–41
tipping attendants, 20
Sneak routes, for traffic avoidance, 34–36
Southeast Las Vegas, map of, 11
Southwest Las Vegas, map of, 9
Spas, best hotels for, 77
Spellbound, 111
Splash, 112
Sports bars, 119
Sports betting, best casino for, 136
Steve Wyrick, World-Class Magician, 112–13
Stratosphere Tower, 63, 94–95, 149–50
Strip (Las Vegas Boulevard)
commuting to/from, 27–29
lodging in, 23–25, 27–28, 30–34
map of, 7
traffic on, 34–36
Strip shows, 124–25
Swimming, 14, 77, 153

Taxes, for shows, 83
Taxis
at airport, 15
to Convention Center, 44
time between locations, 27–29
tipping for, 19–20

Temperatures, seasonal, 14
Tennis, best hotels for, 77
Tickets, for shows, 83–86
Tipping, 19–20, 87–88
Topless bars and shows, 118, 120, 121, 124–25
Tour operators, reservations through, 39–40, 42
Tournament of Kings, 113–14
Traffic, 34–36
Transportation
at airport, 15–18
to Convention Center, 44
free, 29, 31
to shows, 86
Travel agents, 18, 38–39
Travel packages. *See* Package deals

University of Las Vegas, distances to lodgings, 27–29

Video poker
best casino for, 135
house advantage in, 128–29
rules of, 141–42
Views, 76–77, 149–50
Visitor guides, 12–13

Weather, 13
Web sites, information on, 13
Wheel of fortune, 128–29
Wholesale room brokers, 39–40, 42
Wyrick, Steve, magic show, 112–13

Zones of Las Vegas, 5–12. *See also* Downtown; Strip (Las Vegas Boulevard)

2000 *Unofficial Guide* **Reader Survey**

If you would like to express your opinion about Las Vegas or this guide-book, complete the following survey and mail it to:

> 2000 *Unofficial Guide* Reader Survey
> PO Box 43673
> Birmingham AL 35243

Inclusive dates of your visit: _____

Members of your party:	Person 1	Person 2	Person 3	Person 4	Person 5
Gender:	M F	M F	M F	M F	M F
Age:					

How many times have you been to Las Vegas? _____
On your most recent trip, where did you stay? _____

Concerning your accommodations, on a scale of 100 as best and 0 as worst, how would you rate:

The quality of your room?   The value of your room?
The quietness of your room?   Check-in/check-out efficiency?
Shuttle service to the parks?   Swimming pool facilities?

Did you rent a car?   From whom?

Concerning your rental car, on a scale of 100 as best and 0 as worst, how would you rate:

Pick-up processing efficiency?   Return processing efficiency?
Condition of the car?   Cleanliness of the car?
Airport shuttle efficiency?

Favorite restaurants in Las Vegas: _____

_____

Did you buy this guide before leaving?   while on your trip?

How did you hear about this guide? (check all that apply)

Loaned or recommended by a friend   Radio or TV
Newspaper or magazine   Bookstore salesperson
Just picked it out on my own   Library

What other guidebooks did you use on this trip? And on a scale of 100 as best and 0 as worst, how would you rate them? _____

_____

Using the same scale, how would you rate *The Unofficial Guide(s)?* _____